ZEN

AROUND

the

WORLD

ZEN

AROUND

the

WORLD

A 2500-Year Journey
from the Buddha *to* You

by Annellen M. Simpkins, Ph.D., &

C. Alexander Simpkins, Ph.D.

CHARLES E. TUTTLE CO., INC.

BOSTON • RUTLAND, VERMONT • TOKYO

First published in 1997 by Tuttle Publishing, an imprint of Periplus Editions (HK) Ltd., with editorial offices at 153 Milk Street, Boston, Massachusetts 02109.

Library of Congress Cataloging-in-Publication Data

Simpkins, Annellen M.
    Zen around the world : A 2500-Year Journey from the Buddha to you / by Annellen M. Simpkins & C. Alexander Simpkins.
        p.   cm.
    Includes bibliographical references.
    ISBN 0-8048-3082-7
    1. Zen Buddhism—History. 2. Spiritual life—Zen Buddhism.
    I. Simpkins, Alexander. II. Title.
    BQ9262.3.S56   1997
    294.3'927'09—dc21   97-5564
                                                                    CIP

Distributed by

USA
Charles E. Tuttle Co., Inc.
RR 1 Box 231-5
North Clarendon, VT 05759
tel.: (800) 526-2778
fax.: (800) FAX-TUTL

Japan
Tuttle Shokai Ltd.
1-21-13, Seki
Tama-ku, Kawasaki-shi
Kanagawa-ken, 214
Japan
tel.: (044) 833-0225
fax.: (044) 822-0413

Southeast Asia
Berkeley Books Pte. Ltd.
5 Little Road #08-01
Singapore 536983
tel.: (65) 280-3320
fax.: (65) 280-6290

Design by Jill Winitzer
Cover design by Kathryn Sky-Peck

First Edition
05 04 03 02 01 00 99 98 97   1 3 5 7 9 10 8 6 4 2

Printed in the United States of America

We dedicate this book to
our parents, Carmen and Nat Simpkins
and Naomi and Herbert Minkin, and
to our children, Alura Simpkins and
Alex Simpkins.

We wish to thank Isabelle Bleecker,
Michael Kerber, Kathryn Sky-Peck,
Steve Lamont, and Kathleen King, who
helped us "Keep the golden mean
between saying too much and too little"
(Publilius Syrus, 42 B.C.).

CONTENTS

INTRODUCTION

We cannot grasp the formless form

Of the Oneness we are seeing

Emptiness is the inner nature

Within the outer form of being

—*C. Alexander Simpkins*

AS WATER HAS BEEN PRIMARY TO THE LIFE OF THE earth, Zen has been fundamental to the spiritual vitality of the world. Zen inspires us to awaken to a deeper feeling about life. It touches the hearts of humankind everywhere to bestow upon us a profound experience of our own nature, as being at one with the universe. How has this come about and what will evolve?

Novices often have little understanding of the multi-faceted history and complex evolution of Zen as it continues to flow on its journey to many countries and cultures over the centuries. Now that Zen has traveled to the West, we can expect a new interaction that compounds the pragmatic with the spiritual, giving new meaning to Zen. Zen can be expressed and enhanced through everyday life, in work and play, in art and sports; it transforms the mundane into the sublime, the temporal into the eternal. The human mind becomes one with its inner spirit, refreshed with the waters of Zen.

ABOUT THIS BOOK

ZEN AROUND THE WORLD PRESENTS ZEN'S JOURNEY, not simply as a history, but as a spiritual odyssey. Gathered together in this one volume is the entire story of Zen, from its inception to the present day. The story unfolds before you, as Zen's spirit travels across time and place, circling the globe. From its early origins in India, Zen evolved as it spread through China, Korea, and Japan. Its influence now extends beyond the East into Europe and America.

This book offers an intellectual foundation for understanding Zen's passage around the world. Experiential exercises follow, to help you gain a clearer understanding of what makes Zen so relevant to us today. *Zen Around the World* points directly to the Zen spirit that shines like a beacon in the night to show the Way.

Each chapter in Part One focuses on a different area of the world that was touched by Zen. We begin with Zen's origins in India and follow its development through China, Japan, and Korea. Early influences and background philosophies in each country are the setting for Zen. Traditional Zen legends exemplify Zen's spirit and have added depth and inspiration through the ages. The past twenty-five hundred years have seen many great Zen leaders and numerous Zen sects evolve. We have to be selective in our presentation: there are always many more. Historical development embraced diversity, even conflict. Yet through it all, the *spirit* of Zen is always present when Zen is practiced. Understanding the fundamental doctrines and key people of the past will help you bring the basic concepts of Zen to life. You will learn many of the important distinctions between different schools of Zen and share in classic teachings and basic concepts expressed through the ages and across continents.

Part Two brings you to the modern era, as Zen made its transition to the West. Scholars and teachers helped communicate Zen, while the Beats of the 1950s added their own interpretation. Zen found its way into everyday life in such areas as art, sports, activism, and psychotherapy. Clearly Zen's influence has been broad, as Zen has found a meaningful home in many facets of Western life.

Finally, Part Three introduces you to the Zen experience with exercises drawn from the great traditions of the past and modern innovations of the present. Try the exercises. They will help you gain a personal experience of Zen. And may the spirit of Zen inspire you in meaningful ways.

ONENESS
COMES
from
SOMETHING

To mix metaphors, India was the woman, China the man,
Zen the wonderful child.

—R. H. Blyth

MOST SCHOLARS AGREE THAT ZEN WAS BORN from a spiritual interaction between the Indian and Chinese people. The Chinese interpreted the enlightenment of the Buddha from their practical, Taoist orientation. The interweaving of three influences—Yoga, Taoism, and Buddhism—helped create modern Zen, to be transmitted from the Buddha to you.

CHAPTER ONE

Awakening to Oneness: Zen Origins

BUDDHISM'S ROOTS MUST BE TRACED BACK TO EARLIER than the original enlightenment of Prince Siddhartha Gautama, back to the Yogis of India.

•

Indian Yoga Roots

India has always been a spiritually-minded country, concerned with higher consciousness. At a time when many civilizations were only just discovering language and tools, India, with its long-established civilization, already had an advanced language and literature with complex systems of spiritual practice. Early roots of Zen can be found in Indian philosophical writings such as the Upanishads, which date back to 5000 B.C. The Upanishads are a collection of verses that the Hindus regard as holy scriptures. Numerous practices of *dhyana,* or meditation, were practiced throughout India for thousands of years. The practice of Yoga crystallized out from this and evolved as a disciplined method of focusing attention and clearing the mind to achieve union with the universe.

There are many paths of Yoga (such as Hatha Yoga, Gnani Yoga, Bhakti Yoga, Karma Yoga, Mantra Yoga), each emphasizing different techniques and forms of practice. Meditation as the pathway to enlightenment is the common thread that connects them all.

Meditation as the pathway to enlightenment is the link between Yoga and Zen.

Yoga is a method of personal discipline. The word *Yoga* means "union," "the uniting of the self with the universe." Through the practice of Yoga, Yogis seek *samadhi*—enlightenment—when they withdraw their minds from involvement with externals to focus on higher consciousness. Breathing is considered the doorway to control of the mind. Many Yogic meditation exercises use rhythmic breathing to take control of the body, mind, and vital energy, called *prana.* Prana is to Hindu philosophy what *chi* is to the Chinese: an all-pervading principle of life force and energy.

Yoga provides methods to regulate and control the mind in order to attain a peaceful state and achieve self-control, powers, and knowledge. The influence of Yoga on Zen not only can be seen in its emphasis on meditation but also can be traced through some of the Yogic literature, such as the aphorisms of Patanjali that were translated into Chinese. Meditative sects of Yoga integrated with Buddhism, adding meditative disciplines to Buddhism.

Tao-an, one of the greatest Chinese scholar-monks of the fourth century, edited and wrote commentaries on Yogic texts. He interpreted Yoga's meditative state—*dhyana*—in terms of Chinese Taoist philosophy. In the introduction to one of his translations, he points out that the various stages in the control of the breath aim at the gradual diminution of mental activity in order to attain the state of nonactivity. He further explains that Yoga includes a practical set of techniques that the Chinese could use to reach the Taoist ideal of nonactivity and freedom from desire. Undoubtedly, these early translations influenced the Chinese to integrate Yoga, Buddhism, and Taoism in the creation of Ch'an, or Zen.

•

Chinese Taoism: Oneness Is the Tao

Taoism has been a part of Chinese society for more than 1,500 years. During the "warring states" period (481–221 B.C.), many people despaired of ever seeing any end to the violence and chaos of the political and social situation. Taoism offered hope for a better way.

The goal in Taoism is to become one with the spirit of the Tao, the universal Oneness that encompasses everything. When people seek to follow the true nature of things instead of contending or fighting against this nature, they find peace and harmony, and matters resolve effortlessly. The entire thrust of Taoist theory is toward a universal, spiritual principle that we are all a part of and yet lies beyond us: the Tao. Taoists seek to yield to an experience of unity with the Tao for inspiration and guidance, whereas Yogis and Buddhists find answers within, using their own mind. The Tao is the spiritual way of things, the source of meaning. When people stay with this unity and spirit of things, they gain wisdom, sensitivity, and insight. The Tao brings about the union of opposites, the yin and the yang. Taoists seek balance, to include both sides, to be unified in the wholeness that is the Tao. In this union, there is harmony.

The Taoist sage stepped outside active participation in the affairs of man. Instead, he took the path of noninterference to allow the natural course of events to take place. As the Taoists would say, the value of a vase is not of the vase itself but of the empty space it encloses.

"The value of a vase is not of the vase itself but of the empty space it encloses."

The Taoist sage did not believe in acquiring knowledge, possessions, or position. Instead, his goal was to give up everything and become one with the infinite (the Tao) in order to find happiness, fulfillment, and true wisdom. Using this philosophy, the Taoist sages encouraged rulers to govern with less tyranny. To the Taoists, the true nature of humanity is inherently good just as it is. In this way, Taoism differs from other philosophies, such as Confucianism, which seeks to train and discipline people to enhance the expression of human goodness by practice. Taoism believes in bringing out the latent goodness in humanity by releasing people from training, discipline, and practice. When people are in tune with the Tao, they become virtuous naturally. All people have a tendency to be in balance. The expression "go with the flow" derives from Taoist philosophy.

In the third and fourth centuries B.C., Taoism offered a viable alternative to Confucianism. Confucian theory set moral standards for everyday life and conduct that structured and permeated Chinese society, but it did not address the mystical side of humanity. Taoism filled this void, joining with the ancient cults to give the Chinese a fuller, tranquil religious life. Later, Taoism also promised immortality through elixirs and meditation practices.

Taoism attracted poets and scholars who found Confucian doctrine unsatisfying and Taoism's mysterious, poetical guides to conduct, a release. When Buddhism arrived in China between the first and fourth centuries A.D., it was easily adapted into Chinese philosophy, partly because the people had integrated the concept of Taoism. Renunciation of worldly affairs, a positive view of humanity, and harmony with a universal Way had been familiar concepts to the Chinese for close to a thousand years. Buddhist concepts were similar. The Chinese came to accept them as old friends.

•

The Birth of Buddhism in India

Buddhism was born from the enlightenment of one man, Siddhartha Gautama. Siddhartha was born a prince in India, during the sixth century B.C. He led what appeared to be a perfect life, with every luxury one could want, within the palace walls that protected him from any unpleasantness. Yet he carried within him a deep restlessness. Legend has it that one day he traveled outside the palace without his father's permission, with his faithful servant Channah. By accident he chanced upon a sickly man racked with fever and wasting away from starvation. Siddhartha, who had never seen anyone in such pain, asked, "Why does he suffer so?"

His servant answered, "This is the way of life, sire. Many suffer with illness."

Later, they came upon an old man, weak and dying.

Siddhartha asked again, "Why does he suffer so?"

And his servant responded tenderly, "Sire, old age and death are the way of all life. We all must die."

Siddhartha returned home deeply troubled. Feeling called upon to solve the universal problem of suffering, he vowed to leave the comfort of his life in the palace to find the answers for his people. He joined the forest ascetics, who believed that the path to truth and wisdom was through self-denial. Siddhartha starved and disciplined himself, meditating in the woods. He grew weaker and weaker and felt his mental faculties slipping away. As he neared death from starvation, he was suddenly struck by the fact that he could no longer think and was on the verge of death without actually having resolved anything. He realized that this extreme path would never lead him to solve life's difficulties. He knew that, because of his solemn commitment, he must not allow himself to die without succeeding in his quest. Therefore, at that moment, he decided to eat and drink to regain his strength. His fellow monks disapproved, offended. This was not the ascetic way. They chastised him and left him alone in the woods.

Siddhartha returned to pure meditation, determined to reach understanding. He sat under a Bodhi tree, deep in meditation. The first night he was besieged with doubts, agonies, and pains. He remembered his former life of luxury and was tempted to return to it. But his driving urge to solve the problem of suffering prevented him from going back. As the light of dawn lit the horizon, he underwent a profound enlightenment. He felt calm. Answers to the fundamental problems of life seemed clear. He was thirty-five years old.

He felt tempted to remain withdrawn from worldly involvement, content in his own happiness and calm state. Then he experienced a deep compassion for humanity and left his seclusion. Beginning in the city of Benares, in present-day India, he traveled around for forty years, speaking, drawing followers, communicating his message of release from suffering. Soon even kings were meeting with him to learn how to find enlightenment. Monasteries were founded throughout India to teach Siddhartha Gautama's principles.

He explained to his fellow ascetics, "I remember when a crabapple was my only daily food. I was near death, and yet I came no closer to knowledge." He preached, "Avoid the two extremes, luxury and asceticism. Take the Middle Path, a path which opens the eyes and bestows understanding, which leads to peace of mind, to higher wisdom, to full enlightenment, to nirvana!" Even today the Middle Path is a central value in Buddhism. And meditation is the means by which to find it.

Siddhartha discovered answers to his questions about human suffering. He explained that whoever recognizes the existence of suffering, its cause, its remedy, and its cessation has fathomed the Four Noble Truths. They will walk on the right path. The first truth is the recognition that in life, there is suffering: from old age, illness, failure. Second, the cause of suffering is vain, passionate craving. Cravings for being, for nonbeing, for sensual pleasures, and for power are some of the sources of suffering. Third, the cause can be eliminated

"Avoid the two extremes, luxury and asceticism. Take the Middle Path, a path which opens the eyes and bestows understanding, which leads to peace of mind, to higher wisdom, to full enlightenment, to nirvana!"

Shakyamuni Buddha

by renunciation of craving. Finally, the way to accomplish this end is by following the Eightfold Path: right views, right aspirations, right speech, right behavior, right livelihood, right effort, right thoughts, and right contemplation. These eight doctrines, or directives, state clearly the lifestyle required.

Following his enlightenment experience, Siddhartha was given the name Shakyamuni Buddha, meaning the Awakened One. He taught that enlightenment is the result of what we think. He told people that it is vital to tame the mind. Even though it is difficult to restrain the mind from jumping around, seemingly with a will of its own, only a tamed mind brings happiness. Through meditation, people can learn to conquer the self. The enlightenment of Buddha made Zen possible. Buddha-mind is primary to all Zen Buddhists.

Buddha reached thousands of avid followers in his lifetime, but the Zen tradition began when he mysteriously passed along the essence of his teaching without words to one disciple, Mahakasyapa. One bright morning Buddha was addressing his disciples, who listened carefully to every word. As the lecture drew to a close, Buddha held up a single flower. Of all who were gathered, only Mahakasyapa smiled. At that moment, Mahakasyapa received direct transmission, thus marking the legendary beginning of all Zen lineages. Mahakasyapa became Buddha's dharma heir, the first in the line of succession.

Buddha's insights have been passed down through hundreds of generations. But according to legend, Buddha's teachings might have died with him had it not been for Mahakasyapa. Mahakasyapa was traveling at the time of Buddha's death. Along the way he overheard two monks talking. One said, "Buddha's death is not a time for sorrow but is cause for rejoicing. Now that he is gone, we can do exactly what we want without his constant advice and criticism!" On hearing this, Mahakasyapa realized that Buddha's teachings and precepts for living must be compiled and written down if his message was to survive.

Mahakasyapa gathered all the disciples together after Buddha died, for the First Buddhist Council, about 480 B.C. Ananda, one of Buddha's devoted disciples, possessed an unusually sharp memory. He had remembered every sermon and could repeat every word. During the meeting, Ananda recited all the sermons, precepts, and ordinances. He began each sermon with the words "Thus have I heard," and this is how all the earliest Buddhist sutras open. The council verified (by the collective memory of all present) the correctness of their recollections, and the first sutras were recorded. Eventually sermons preached by the disciples were added, along with commentaries. Other councils were convened and more sutras were gathered, all supposedly from Buddha's direct teachings. It was not until three hundred years later, as the memory of the Buddha himself was fading, that many new sutras were written, beginning a new tradition.

Early Buddhist Sects: The Old Wisdom Schools

India nurtured Buddha's religion. As the years passed, the teachings were interpreted in diverse ways. Numerous, sometimes conflicting, variations of Buddhism evolved, eventually dividing into the many sects that flourish today. The Old Wisdom School, now known as Hinayana, was the first school of Buddhism, forming into two divisions about two hundred years after the death of Buddha. The eastern division, known as Theravada, spread successfully throughout Southeast Asia in Sri Lanka, Myanmar (Burma), and Thailand, where it is still strong. In the West, the Savastivadins were the main philosophical school of Buddhism. The philosophies of the other Old Wisdom sects have vanished, their teachings lost to the mists of time.

The Old Wisdom Schools sought the perfecting of the spirit through becoming an *arhat,* a saint. Nirvana was to be reached by each individual. This early form of Buddhism required the ascetic denial of one's worldly life. The *sangha,* the community of Buddha's followers, became co-owners of all property and goods. Each individual monk was allowed only a few essential possessions, such as a robe and a bowl. The sect depended on donations from the kings. When a monastery was donated, the sangha gradually grew. Monks followed the Buddha's carefully thought-out set of concepts, the Four Noble Truths and the Eightfold Path, that explained the cause of suffering and how one could be released from the cycle of suffering (*samsara*). Following Buddha's Way led logically to the peaceful state of nirvana. The ascetic lifestyle required that seekers achieve the goalless goal: nirvana through renunciation.

The Old Wisdom view conceptualized the perfected seeker as one with the emptiness. The sangha required constant mindfulness in meditation, called *vipassana*: holding the attention firmly to the details of the body, sensations, and actions just as they are. Attention was paid to training the mental states, which were viewed as reflections of the mind's grasping. Once practitioners realized this, they could reject all discriminations of consciousness as delusory, negative forms of attachment to this transitory life; only then could one gain release from suffering. The directives of the scriptures are clear: turn away from concern for and experience of the world through the senses, feelings, and mind. The world is an illusion, a temptation to cravings for apparent pleasures and the inevitable sufferings from its transitoriness. Cravings lead to delusions and discomforts. Freedom from the craving for this is liberating, and leads the practitioner to be truly happy.

Buddhism taught that the world is an illusion.

Consider that your body is only a collection of fluids, blood, urine, tissues, and so on. Then you are not drawn to identify with it and consequently long for its pleasures. This is how concentration and meditation were used in early Old Wisdom Buddhism. Monks were encouraged to view their bodies and senses as merely transitory illusions, even as disgusting. This ascetic lifestyle required all desire to be extinguished so that the quest for nirvana could become the central focus for seekers. Meaningfulness was not to be found in everyday life in the material world but rather in nirvana. Perfecting the spirit took precedence.

Enlightenment and nirvana were reserved for only the committed monks. Lay monks were less common, since austere discipline was required for monks to stay within the order. The customs and needs of the working-class people were not addressed by this approach.

Mahayana Buddhism: The New Wisdom Schools

As time passed, other philosophical implications of Buddhism gradually became clear to the intellectually active, leading to a new form of Buddhism: Mahayana. By the first century A.D., Mahayana Buddhism diverged subtly from the early sects and followed another route, celebrating the Buddha Way with ritual, ceremony, deep philosophical theory, and, in some sects, worship through pageantry. As Mahayana spread throughout Asia, the indigenous beliefs and customs of the people were included, thereby making the practice of Buddhism comprehensible and more palatable to the general population.

The Old Wisdom Schools of Buddhism had moved apart because of contentions about doctrine and practice. Despite these differences, many hoped Buddhism could remain united. The Second Buddhist Council, held at Vaisali approximately one hundred years after Buddha's death, attempted to purify the teachings. The general consensus of the council was to unify. However, arguments over differences continued. The Third Council was convened in 250 B.C. at Pataliputra by King Asoka, the great Indian benefactor and proponent of Buddhism. He and his family spread Buddhism throughout India (and beyond) and tried to resolve the growing differences between sects. But differences continued to grow.

One of the fundamental splits was between a conservative Old Wisdom School, the Sthavira School, and an innovative dissenting Old Wisdom group called the Mahasanghikas. The south of India was a sanctuary for the Mahasanghikas, who began formally around 250 B.C. This larger group gradually diversified into smaller groups led by brilliant thinkers who compounded the assumptions of Buddhism with their own interpretations. They formulated new doctrines and contemplated the implications. These groups were the forerunners of the schools of the Mahayana, the New Wisdom Schools.

The Mahasanghikas criticized traditional Buddhism for not being a true religion. Early Buddhism included a set of atheistic practices. The early dissenting sects tried to rectify the deficiencies they saw in the strict, narrow codes. They relaxed the monastic rules, created rituals, worshipped the Buddha, appealed to the imagination of the people, and addressed their real-life concerns. Mahayana offered a different group identity, which included many ways of life as legitimate for the seeker and lay practitioner. Their ideal was not the arhat—the perfected being—but the Bodhisattva, a selfless individual who compassionately refuses nirvana until all are saved. Since all are part of the Oneness, all must realize their intrinsic Buddha-nature for complete Oneness. Everyone must help one another, for when one is helped, all are helped.

The Buddhism of the Mahayana did evolve to become a religion rather than remain as a set of practices. Elaborate rituals, ceremonies, and complex theoretical interpretations became an integral part of Mahayana Buddhist doctrine.

Mahayana also accepted the transfer of merit by donation, including statues and property. The Old Wisdom School disapproved. Tensions were inevitable.

With the continuing tension between tradition and innovation, Old Wisdom Schools and New Wisdom Schools were both ready to recognize their differences and formally divided at the Fourth Council (around the second century A.D.) into Hinayana and Mahayana, a division that we now take for granted in describing Buddhism.

Hinayana attempted to distinguish itself from the indigenous religion of Hinduism. By contrast, the Mahayana flexibly combined with the people's traditional beliefs and gods, reinstating such Hindu concepts as reincarnation, karma, deities, and heaven and hell. The Buddhist deities were essentially Hindu deities recast. A pantheon of lesser and greater gods, as guardian Buddhas, was instituted. In the new view, Siddhartha Gautama was thought of as only one of a series of Buddhas, past and future, and earth as only one of many dimensions, both lower and higher. The Mahayana theorists were optimistic about the human condition, asserting that many paths can lead to enlightenment and that this life can be a springboard to the pool of nirvana's wisdom. On the other hand, the Hinayana believed that millions of years (*kalpas*) of striving by the individual monk were necessary to reach nirvana. They condescended to lay followers and therefore shut out the ordinary person, who might lack the patience that such a belief requires.

Vishnu, a Hindu deity.

Hinayana schools acknowledged only the sutras allegedly spoken by the Buddha or his direct disciples as his true voice. The Mahayana changed this view, casting the Buddha into a new role as the inner spirit of the universe, incarnated in human form from time to time. Mahayana philosophy embraced a notion of the Buddha as a timeless, ineffable, godlike spirit. Therefore, other sutras written long after Siddhartha Gautama's death could be accepted and included as valid expressions of the Buddha-mind. This conception was more creative and less a cult of the person that limited the doctrine to Siddhartha's personally delivered sermons and statements.

Mahayana's development drew from two important early schools of philosophy, whose echoes still resonate through modern Zen Buddhism: Nagarjuna's Madhyamikans and the Yogacaras.

Nagarjuna: The Middle Way

Madhyamika, the Middle Way philosophy, was founded by Nagarjuna in the second century A.D. Chinese and Japanese scholars often credit him as being the founder of Mahayana Buddhism. He was an Indian monk, philosopher, and logician who reputedly lived for three hundred years. This legend alone shows the great esteem in which he was held as a wise elder. Nagarjuna presented logical propositions that demonstrated the self-contradictory nature of all possible assertions about the nature of reality. Following Nagarjuna's logical discourse, the doctrine of *sunyata,* or emptiness, was proposed—a concept that cannot even be called by name, lest it lose its empty nature by being named! Nagarjuna demonstrated logically that since nothing has "independent origination," everything has an inner emptiness of any individual self-nature. Since everything is relative to this inner emptiness, as well as being linked to everything else, logically nothing exists in and of itself. All is ultimately empty, devoid of outer existence or any inner nature. This was a forerunner of the modern philosophy of relativism, though with a different application.

All is ultimately empty, devoid of outer existence or any inner nature.

In Nagarjuna's theory, the universe is codependent. It originates in a linked chain. No part exists outside its relationship to the whole, which defines its existence; thus, nothing really exists in itself. The paradox is thus: all is empty, yet all exists. Emptiness as a concept coexists with fullness. Each is defined by virtue of the other, as a background context for contrast, its opposite in meaning.

As an analogy, an automobile requires wheels, a body, an engine, seats, and all its parts (or at least, most of them) to exist and function as a car, yet no one part in itself is a car. A set of wheels, a motor, a steering wheel—none of these parts alone is a car, as any auto parts supplier will assure you. A car is dependent on its component parts to exist as a unity, yet the parts become a car only when all are bolted together in synthesis. The car comes into being when they compound together, through their interrelationship. They are interrelated and codependent.

Being itself exists in relation to nonbeing. Without nonbeing for contrast, we cannot define being. Nirvana and samsara are both illusions, existing only through contrast to the other, threads within the tapestry of appearances. [1]

Nothing cannot even be called "nothing," either, lest it becomes something by the very naming within the definition. This leaves us with the Middle Way—neither one nor the other, both, yet not both—a paradox of logic. The mind-set of the koan in later Zen derives from Nagarjuna's paradoxical logic. [2]

Nagarjuna detailed and elucidated this philosophy of emptiness into a position that he called "the Middle Way," based on this rationale of paradox. Nagarjuna's theory used a philosophical equivalent of the mathematical concept of the zero point—the midpoint on a number line between positive and negative integers—to remain faithful to the concept of reality that was the product of early Buddhist epistemology. The Middle Path also became fundamental to the basic philosophical position about reality in Zen.

Nagarjuna's philosophy negated all the possible pairs of opposites by demonstrating that they are untenable logically. Nonbeing and being, both and neither, are all demonstrated to be untenable philosophical positions concerning ultimate reality. Subsequent Mahayana theories held that one or the other is paramount, as the sutra section will detail. The Middle Path is the ultimate basis for Mahayana, based on Buddha's personal discovery of the Middle Way.

Yogacara

Another early sect of Buddhism that diverged from the original Old Wisdom School was the Yogacaras, also known as the Consciousness School. The Yogacara believed in the primacy of Yogic meditation. Like Nagarjuna, they were the counterpart of the wisdom schools, believing that the mind, by philosophy, can be encouraged to give up attempting to think conceptually and therefore derive insight. Adherents of Yogacara sought to find enlightenment through the calm of meditation.

The founder of the Yogacara School was Maitreyanatha, (A.D. 270–350). By the fourth century, two brothers named Asanga and Vasubandu took the theory further, developing the Yogacara School known as Vijnanavada. These philosophers argued that in Buddhist philosophy all objects exist only in the mind: mind alone is real; objects have no actual reality outside it. This was a forerunner of twentieth-century European phenomenology. Madhyamika philosophy emphasized thought as the method to higher knowledge, but the Yogacaras held that meditation is the key; therefore, it is more logical to emphasize meditation and consciousness. Only through consciousness, correctly applied, can true insight be experienced. Yoga is the science of meditation.

The Yogacara conceptualized the mind as having hierarchical levels of consciousness, the highest level being that of a kind of collective unconscious, the principle of the absolute as a storehouse of the seeds of reality, created by karmic deeds. The Yogacara were careful to specify that it is a mistake to attempt to mentally hold onto any conception of these levels of consciousness. Conceptions are intended to function as a map, to orient the mind toward the source of the *state* of consciousness, not toward any particular idea or concept itself. The idea simply serves as a kind of mental scaffolding, to allow the practitioner access to levels of meditative trance that are systematically abstracted from involvement with the deceptive world of the senses and involvement with consciousness of objects. The Yogacara considered the apparent objective world of reality to be only an appearance, a mere magic show, a performance of illusions that are actually taking place in consciousness. The practice of meditation, guided by their map, is the means to freedom from enchantment by illusion's spell.

These views were basic in casting the theoretical foundation that Mahayana was based on. These concepts articulated a nonconceptual reality of experience that is now taken for granted as a basis for thousands of writings in the Mahayana scriptures. The *sutras* and *sastras*—narratives and treatises—paradoxically cannot express reality's character in words, yet they use words affirmatively to point to it, to help seekers to directly experience reality. Like van Gogh's beautiful expressive paintings of his experience of people and landscapes, these scriptures in themselves have become objects of reverence. Echoes of the implications of these concepts, with corresponding emphases, resonate throughout the centuries like ripples in a lake, through thousands of writings in the Mahayana literature.

These concepts articulated a nonconceptual reality of experience that is now taken for granted as a basis for Mahayana.

Later Mahayana sects in China, such as the T'ien-t'ai and the Hua Yen, synthesized and combined the emphases of both Madhyamika and Yogacara, including both philosophical insight and the practice of meditation as part of the path to enlightenment.

Tantric Buddhism

The Yogacara, with their conceptual maps to point the way to transcend the everyday world in meditation, had a profound influence on Zen Buddhism. They also set the stage for Tantric Buddhism, the last of the Mahayana sects that flourished in India before Buddhism was debated philosophically and reabsorbed into the melting pot of Hinduism. Then Buddhism vanished from its place of origin.

Tantric Buddhism was a new form of Mahayana Buddhism that is still practiced today in modified form in Tibetan Buddhism and, to a lesser extent, is part of the Mahayana canon. The Tantric sects combined beliefs and conceptions from Hatha Yoga and indigenous shamanic and mystical traditions with Buddhist cosmology to create techniques for the development of higher consciousness. Under the guidance of a *guru,* or master, the practitioner used visualization, chanting of *mantras,* concentration on diagrams known as *mandalas,* secret rituals and ceremonies, and other meditative methods to focus and direct practitioners on the quest for nirvana. Tantric Buddhism included the teacher as a guru, a special guide to higher consciousness.

Tantric Buddhism divided into many sects, but two main branches formed: Tsung-mi, or School of Secrets, and the Vajrayana, or Adamantine Vehicle. Tantric practitioners believed that esoteric powers bordering on the supernatural can be gained by Yogic meditation combined with Buddhist concepts. One well-documented ability was adepts' learning to generate psychic heat; as a result, they could actually raise their body temperature at will, defying extreme physical conditions. The test to show that adepts had acquired this advanced skill required them to melt the snow around them and even to dry cold, wet towels placed across their shoulders and backs in subzero weather! This power could help wandering pilgrims survive the freezing Himalayas. Other abilities may be less well documented, but scientifically, many practical applications for meditation have been detailed.

The School of Secrets was conservative and philosophical, using symbolic visualization combined with mantras, chanting, and mandalas to raise consciousness. The Adamantine Vehicle included some extremely liberal practices that were not always acceptable to the status quo—in that through challenging social limits and norms, practitioners could weaken the hold of all limiting norms of delusion over them. Social rebellion, symbolic sexual practices, and behavioral extremes thereby paradoxically became a source of inspiration for transcendence and enlightenment.

Tantra was the last development of Buddhism before it largely disappeared from India. The School of Secrets became part of Shingon and Tendai Buddhism in Japan and has had an influence on present-day Korean Buddhism. The Adamantine Vehicle found its way into smaller movements and cults.

•

Indian Buddhism Comes to China

Buddhism has been one of the most pervasive foreign influences on China. Its importance is comparable to the introduction of Christianity into the West. No doubt, China was transformed by Buddhism, but the Chinese people, with their unique philosophical background, had an equally profound effect on Buddhism, transforming it into a uniquely Chinese religion.

Why did Buddhism capture the imagination and spirit of the Chinese people?

Why did Buddhism, which seems at first glance to be so utterly foreign to the practical Chinese mind, capture the imagination and spirit of its people? The answer can be found at many levels of Chinese society, from personality to politics.

Buddhism filled some serious voids that existed in Chinese religion and philosophy. Confucianism offered moral and ethical guidelines for daily life, but little nourishment for the people's spiritual side. Taoism did deal with mystical Oneness of the Tao but, as a religion, tended to lack goals and guides to ethical conduct sufficient for the general population. The promise of immortality was open only to those who became sophisticated in the intricate combinations of herbology, alchemy, and philosophy.

Mahayana Buddhism was a religion that welcomed everyone. No matter how humble, uneducated, or even formerly immoral—anyone could share in salvation. Mahayana offered explicit guides for morality and a rationale for peaceful unity. Also, the promise for an afterlife was certainly better than this life, and this promise offered hope to the poor, hardworking masses.

Most important, Mahayana Buddhism continued to be adaptable, allowing the Chinese to keep many of their traditional Taoist and Confucian beliefs. They could continue to worship their old gods and ancestral spirits, recast into new forms and roles. The saying "Three ways to one goal" referred to the combination of Buddhism, Taoism, and Confucianism that many people practiced simultaneously. Even though some assumptions in the three theories were not compatible, each addressed different aspects of life. The same interplay among philosophies occurred in Japan, where, for example, the *samurai* were trained in Confucianism as a guide for ethical conduct while also learning Zen as mental training useful for combat and proper action as warriors, as the Japan section details.

Missionaries came to China by the thousands during the period when Buddhism flowered in India, beginning in the first century A.D. and continuing for hundreds of years. They traveled along well-established trade routes that existed between China and India, coming both by land and by sea. These monks brought with them a zealous religious fervor that was contagious. They carried Buddhism to China and throughout the rest of Asia. Mahayana spread rapidly, evolving further as it was applied to other cultures and contexts. It was enlarged by the interaction with other countries, philosophies, and languages.

Several Indian scholars devoted themselves to translating the sacred texts from Sanskrit to Chinese. Dharmaraksha (A.D. 231–308), who was said to be master of thirty-six languages, translated more than 175 Buddhist works. Kumarajiva (A.D. 344–413) set up a bureau of translation in China, where he supervised hundreds of monks in the translation of ninety-four works into Chinese. These many volumes of sutras, now made intelligible to the general population, impressed the Chinese, who had long held deep respect for the written word.

Kumarajiva's most skillful translation was of the philosophies of Nagarjuna. Through Kumarajiva's teaching more than five hundred students, along with the later work of his disciples, Madhyamika was spread throughout China. Kumarajiva was the key figure in the propagation and evolution of the Madhyamika known in China as the Three Treatises School. Seng Chao (A.D. 374–414), the foremost Chinese disciple of Kumarajiva, did much to promote this doctrine, which later had a fundamental influence on Zen. The three treatises important to the Chinese sect were first, Madhyamika Sastra, or Treatise on the Middle Doctrine; second, Dvadasanikaya Sastra, or Treatise on the Twelve Gates; and third, Aryadeva Sata Sastra, or Treatise on the One Hundred Verses.

With the fall of the Han dynasty (206 B.C.–A.D. 265), China broke up into small, weakened territories that were vulnerable to Mongol invasion. These times of turmoil opened the door to Buddhism. When the Mongols conquered northern China, many Confucian scholars who had been involved with the previous government fled to the south. Buddhist and Taoist scholars remained in the north. The new rulers looked for spiritual advisors, a typical practice of the times. The Mongols chose Buddhist and Taoist scholars whose conduct, philosophies, and mystical practices were congenial to their beliefs. The Buddhist and Taoist advisors helped moderate the fierce ways of the Mongols.

Inspired by their introduction to Buddhism, many Chinese monks made pilgrimages to India to experience this new religion firsthand from its source and view the historical sites. Several Chinese monks who became famous for their travels brought back copies of the ancient sutras. One of these monks, Fa-hsien (A.D. 337–422), set out in 399 to obtain from India perfect copies of the sacred Buddhist texts. He wrote about his adventures in a book, the *Fo-kuo chi*, which has survived today as *The Travels of Fa-hsien*. Upon his return to China in 414, he spent his remaining years translating the many Buddhist classics he had brought home.

During the fourth and fifth centuries, the popularity of Buddhism expanded in the north. There, continual disputes between Taoists and Buddhists were fueled by alternating periods of imperial favor and support, sometimes for one group, sometimes for the other. When Taoists were empowered by the rulers, Buddhists were persecuted; when Buddhists had the royal favor, the Taoists were oppressed. But these persecutions were intermittent and fairly mild. By A.D. 405, nine out of ten Chinese families practiced Buddhism.

Disputes between Taoists and Buddhists were fueled by alternating periods of imperial favor and support.

Over the next hundred years Buddhism spread southward until eventually the entire country embraced the new religion. Southern China's Emperor Liang Wu Ti (502–57) is remembered for his strong support of Buddhism. After having been a devoted Confucianist, he converted to Buddhism in his middle years. Three times he attempted to give up the responsibilities of rule to join the Buddhist monastery himself. Three times his court officials brought the emperor back to his royal duties. Despite opposition from his court, the emperor persisted in his royal patronage and involvement with Buddhism. He became a vegetarian and made animal sacrifices illegal. Through his support, the collection of all Buddhist scriptures, the Tripitaka, was compiled, translated, and published.

Although many Chinese leaders and their people embraced Buddhism, some found certain Buddhist practices to be scandalous. Buddhists were encouraged to give up all family ties and to practice celibacy, which went against the strong Chinese tradition of filial piety. Many felt that breaking up the family was destructive to Chinese culture. Furthermore, religious organizations received many economic benefits (such as relief from taxes and exemption from military service). Thousands joined the monasteries to escape financial responsibility.

Buddhism vied with Taoism and Confucianism, sometimes bitterly, for royal favor, expressed as donations and influence. Consequently, state suppression of Buddhism occurred sporadically, depending on the religious preference of the leader. When Taoist and Confucianist forces gained supremacy, Emperor Wu-tsung felt justified in ordering the obliteration of Buddhism. During the period A.D. 841–45, 40,000 temples and 4,600 monasteries were burned; 256,000 monks and nuns were forced to return to lay life; and millions of acres of tax-exempt temple lands were confiscated. [3] Only Zen survived, because it had remained apart from any state support or involvement.

China made many contributions to Buddhism. Several original Buddhist sects began on Chinese soil and developed a uniquely Chinese character, intertwined with Taoist and Confucianist thought. The Buddhist sects tended to be of two types: gradual and sudden. The Gradual Way was in accord with Confucianism's emphasis on learning as a lifelong pursuit. Sudden-enlightenment sects followed the Taoist orientation, believing that true understanding comes instantly in a sudden flash of intuition, not from preparation, learning, or rational thought. These two themes were later reflected in Zen Buddhism as a point of contention between the northern and southern schools.

T'ien-t'ai Buddhism

T'ien-t'ai Buddhism (Tendai Buddhism in Japanese) bases its tenets on two sutras and a sastra: the Wisdom Sutra, the Lotus Sutra, and Nagarjuna's commentary on the "Long Chapter" of the Wisdom Sutra along with his Madhyamika Sastra. Nagarjuna is considered the First Patriarch, since Hui Wen (d. A.D. 578) became inspired upon reading Nagarjuna's commentary on the Wisdom Sutra. Hui Wen passed along his teachings to Hui-ssu (d. A.D. 577), who became the Third Patriach, followed by Chih-i (A.D. 538–97), the Fourth Patriarch. Chih-i is often remembered as the founder of T'ien-t'ai, possibly because of his many clearly written treatises instructing people on exactly how to follow T'ien-t'ai: *Samatha-Vipasyana for Beginners* (*T'ung Meng Chih Kuan*), *The Six Profound Dharma Doors* (*Lu Miao Fa Meng*), and *The Mahasamatha-vipasyana* (*Mo Ho Chih Kuan*). The T'ien-t'ai Buddhist sect was named for the mountain where Chih-i taught his approach. The lineage continued uninterrupted through the Tenth Patriarch, Tao Sui, who taught Dengya Daishi, who introduced Tendai to Japan in the ninth century.

"Clearing the mind" and "disciplined analysis" are both necessary in T'ien-t'ai.

T'ien-t'ai teaches that Chih and Kuan are the two main conceptual techniques for achieving enlightenment. *Chih* means "clearing the mind" and "holding attention on one thing," *Kuan* means "disciplined analysis," "filling the mind with thought and recollection." Both are necessary, though each has its appropriate use and time of application. Partial practice is wrong, according to Chih-i. Specific techniques of meditation that use both methods are described in T'ien-t'ai, as is a description for their application to the monk's life, not only as a means of realizing enlightenment but also as a guide to conduct and even to heal the body.

The doctrines in the sutras of Buddha were sometimes in conflict with one another. T'ien-t'ai systematized and simplified the complex Buddhist metaphysics into categories of concepts so that the varieties of Buddhism made sense. The T'ien-t'ai sect formulated a philosophy that organizes the apparently inconsistent sutras into a grand hierarchical synthesis. They are all viewed as combined in an algebraic formula. T'ien-t'ai has created a group of categories of an object's suchness (or thusness), form, substance, and cause within ten realms of beings, from demons of hell to Buddhas. Suchness is unaffected by changing modes and is beyond words. All objects are interrelated with one another and with further variables to create three thousand worlds, all are contained in a single thought. Thought is ultimately emptiness, empty of content and form. Meditation is given a definite place, combined with analytic insight through philosophical study, as part of the practice for realizing truth.

These doctrines were the background for Zen Buddhism in Japan, where Tendai had already established itself. T'ien-t'ai doctrines also influenced the Korean Buddhist scholar Chinul, who helped unify Zen and Buddhism in Korea.

Hua-yen School

The Hua-yen School never existed as a separate school in India but became a fairly large movement in China. Based in the Avatamsaka Sutra, the school was said to begin with Tu-shan (557–640), who lectured and wrote about the sutra. The Third Patriarch, Fa-tsang (643–712), did the most to organize and teach Hua-yen. Some consider him the true founder. He wrote more than sixty works explaining Hua-yen philosophy. He was a powerful speaker and lectured widely. "Even the earth shook" when he spoke about the Avatamsaka Sutra, according to an account of a lecture he gave in 699. [4]

The Hua-yen system is similar to T'ien-t'ai, and yet it is more syncretic and all-inclusive. T'ien-t'ai's perfect harmony comes from mutual inclusion of all things. In the Hua-yen school, perfect harmony is more than mutual inclusion; it is also mutual implication. The logic is that emptiness makes this mutual implication possible. Since each individual item is empty and the whole universe is empty, then not only does emptiness include everything but also the individual item, in its emptiness, reflects and shares in the nature of the whole. This is what is meant by interpenetration. (See "The Avatamsaka Sutra," page 38.)

Hua-yen had far-reaching effects over time and place. In Japan the Hua-yen School became known as the Kegon School. Hua-yen was important to Korean Zen as a basis for Chinul's synthesis of the study of traditional Buddhist sutras with Zen's wordless meditation. The teachings of Hua-yen were developed into the Five Ranks during the Chinese Sung period (960–1279) and then incorporated into Hakuin's Rinzai Zen in the eighteenth century. The journey of Zen continued.

Amida Buddhism

Though T'ien-t'ai was popular and powerful, and Hua-yen was comprehensive, they were complex and required much intellectual effort. Neither school was as widely accepted by the general population as the Pure Land (Ch'ing Tu) School was. The founder of this school in China, Hui-yuan (A.D. 334–416), had been a devoted Taoist. He turned to an ancient Indian Buddhist sect that offered passage to paradise through absolute faith in Amitabha, one of the many Buddhas in the spiritual universe of Mahayana lands. People who practice this religion do not have to give up their normal worldly routines. They secure their place in the Pure Land paradise by earnestly calling the name of Amitabha. Believers do so with faith and trust in Amitabha's compassion and devotion as a bodhisattva to save them. One Pure Land sect insisted that even one wholehearted recitation was enough to bring about this salvation. Salvation through simple, unwavering belief in Amitabha Buddha does not require study of sutras or any change in lifestyle, such as taking refuge in a monastery. Pure Land Buddhism offers a simple and accessible pathway: salvation based on pure faith. Unlike Zen and other forms of Buddhism in which one's own efforts are pivotal, in Pure Land, hope, trust, and faith in others hold the key. This appealed to both the Japanese and Chinese. Pure Land Buddhism offers hope to ordinary people who may find it difficult to intellectually comprehend and reach nirvana by their own struggling efforts. Through the efforts of another, the very nature of the bodhisattva vow of a perfect evolved being—Amitabha—they can become enlightened.

Modern theory does not interpret the Pure Land as referring only to a literal geographical place. The colloquial expression "Where you're coming from" expresses what the Amida Buddhists believe. In this form of Buddhism, the pure state of mind becomes the basis for all functioning. Pure Land is this state of mind, of purity and faith. The Pure Land devotee, through his or her state of mind, becomes one with the spirit of the compassionate Buddha as the path. The universe is mind, the mind is Buddha, and earnestly emptying the mind by reciting the name of Buddha creates a clear state of consciousness in the faithful that is open to receiving a Zen-like enlightenment. This approach continues to be popular.

The pure state of mind becomes the basis for all functioning.

Ch'an (Zen)

Zen, called Ch'an in Chinese, was one of the most prominent Chinese sects. Its direct, clear message of salvation achieved through inward enlightenment offers hope for the problems of the human condition. Yet it was to go through many transformations in its evolutionary journey.

•

The Sutras

The sutras are important to the roots of Zen because they provided an intellectual context for the spirit of Zen to emerge and grow. The Sanskrit word *sutra* originally meant "string" or "thread." Sutras were usually collections of short phrases, like threads. The earlier Brahmins had been using sutras to describe their teachings for centuries. Buddhism continued this tradition.

The materials called Buddhist sutras are thought to have derived from the Buddha himself. The first collection of sutras consisted of the original words of Buddha, as recited by Ananda. These sutras were called the Sutra-pitaka, or Sutra Basket. Numerous precepts and monastic rules (*vinaya*) were collected into the Vinaya-pitaka, or Ordinance Basket. The later commentaries on Buddha's sermons were gathered into the Abhidharma-pitaka, or Treatise Basket. These three baskets were brought together into the Tripitaka, or Three Baskets, that make up the main collection of Buddhist literature.

Sutras that were ascribed to the Buddha three to four hundred years before were also recorded, and subsequent editorial changes polished and refined their outer appearance. Some of the sutras aim to persuade readers, often in the form of a dialogue, of the truth of the Buddhist principles. Others are philosophical and abstract writings, pushing the limits of intellectual thought. What follows are some of the most important Buddhist sutras that have been inspirational to Zen masters.

The Lankavatara Sutra

The Lankavatara Sutra was the favorite of Bodhidharma (440–528) to such an extent that at first his sect was known as the Lanka sect. Bodhidharma was said to have given a copy of the Lankavatara Sutra to Hui-k'o (487–593), telling him, "Study the Lankavatara Sutra; it is all you will ever need." This sutra was probably composed about the second century A.D. by the Yogacara School. It was translated into Chinese at various times: in A.D. 420, 443, 513, and 700. The sutra emphasizes the psychological aspects of the process of enlightenment by describing the states of consciousness involved. Through meditation, the practitioner experiences a liberating conversion of consciousness that occurs at the moment of enlightenment. This moment is irrational, with a dropping-away of the usual experience of self into an "unborn state" (like Zen's "original nature before you were born"). Our ordinary consciousness perceives the everyday world as having self-nature, existing by itself. But the enlightened consciousness realizes that all this is illusion. Everything disappears, including the ego or self. There is a revolution, a turning-about of consciousness, a letting-go of illusion, which penetrates to the core of being. All that remains is Absolute Mind, also called the Dharma of Solitude in the sutra.

All that remains is Absolute Mind.

> That all things are in their self-nature unborn, Mahamati, belongs to the realm of self-realization attained by noble wisdom, and does not belong essentially to the realm of dualistic discrimination cherished by the ignorant and simpleminded. [5]

The Lankavatara Sutra uses innumerable comparisons and analogies to illustrate that the perceived world is really our own mind, with no actuality: it is merely an illusion of substance.

The Prajnaparamita Sutra

The Prajnaparamita, Sutra of Perfect Wisdom, is a primary group of sutras for Zen. It is eight thousand lines long and collects many shorter sutras. The main topic throughout is that Buddhist enlightenment leads to perfect wisdom. The attainment of the wisdom of emptiness is esteemed as the highest goal.

"Form is no other than emptiness; emptiness is no other than form."
–from the Heart Sutra

The quality of this wisdom lies beyond words. It is reached through the realization that everything is ultimately empty. Step by step, the reader is led away from worldly perception toward the enlightened state.

> Where there is no perception, appellation, conception or conventional expression, there one speaks of "perfect wisdom." [6]

This state of consciousness is calm and quiet, and is achieved by "no-training." [7] This seemingly paradoxical and confusing direction helps practitioners reach beyond rational logic into the recesses of the unconscious mind. Nonverbal, nonconceptual experience is the heart of perfect wisdom.

The Heart Sutra, the shortest Wisdom Sutra, expresses

the relationship between form and emptiness: form is emptiness, and emptiness is form. The enlightened consciousness, without thought or conception, realizes the ultimate emptiness and impermanence of all things. Yet, through experiencing the myriad things apparent in our everyday lives as mere form, we are able to comprehend emptiness. The two are interrelated, forever linked. The outer vehicle is form, the inner content is emptiness, and thus, paradoxically, nothing is attained when nirvana—the greatest attainment of all—is reached. The Heart Sutra is chanted regularly by most Zen sects. It has virtue as a mantra to clear the mind and inspire.

The Diamond Sutra, written about A.D. 350, is a small book in the Prajnaparamita collection. The original Diamond Sutra is the oldest known book, made up of seven sheets pasted together to form a sixteen-foot scroll. It is still preserved today at the British Museum in London. Said to be passed down orally from Buddha's own words, the Diamond Sutra epitomizes Zen's message of wordless insight beyond thought and reason.

This Mahayana text influenced many later Zen masters, who considered it preeminent among all sutras for Zen. Hui-neng (A.D. 638–713), the Sixth Patriarch and founder of the Southern School of Zen, experienced his enlightenment immediately upon hearing the Diamond Sutra being recited.

In it, Buddha addresses a large assembly of followers through the questions of one of his prominent disciples, Subhuti. Buddha explains that nirvana is open to all who are willing to give up their ego and individuality, since the way of the ego is false. All characteristics are actually no-characteristics. Therefore, people should not be attached to concepts of any kind. To reach enlightenment is to understand that all things are ultimately empty, devoid of intrinsic qualities. Buddhist truth lies beyond the objective world. Seekers of the Buddhist Way must give up their usual modes of thinking and experiencing. Then they will develop a pure, lucid mind that does not depend on sensual perceptions of the world, or even of enlightenment.

To help people discover this state of mind, the sutra presents a paradox: "It neither is nor is not." [8] The Chinese Zen monks sometimes communicated this paradox by bizarre, irrational behavior that was meant to reflect and transmit this state of mind to their students. True attainment comes from a special kind of mental development, but it lacks any actual being or substance. Dharma is like a boat, a raft to cross the river, to be discarded when you reach the other shore. It is a functional reality only, to keep only as long as it is useful.

The sutra closes when Buddha once again beseeches his followers to detach themselves from everyday life:

> Thus shall ye think of all this fleeting world:
> A Star at dawn, a bubble in a stream;
> A flash of lightning in a summer cloud,
> A flickering lamp, a phantom, and a dream. [9]

The Avatamsaka Sutra

The Avatamsaka Sutra is another large collection of works, spanning the first through fourth centuries A.D. These sutras bridge the gap between the Middle Way of Nagarjuna and the Consciousness Only School of the Yogacara. Few comprehend its complex meaning.

The sutra is based on the principle that all objects are interrelated and interpenetrate one another. The universal, the emptiness of nonbeing, is the inner nature, the heart of individual manifestations. Individual manifestations are the expression of the universal. Thus, all are contained in each one, and one is contained in all: they share the same nature. Even the perceiving mind is part of this. Our experience is a function of the apparent world around us. Without something apparent to perceive, we would have no experience. The whole includes its part.

The Third Patriarch of the Hua-yen school, Fa-tsang (A.D. 643–712), was said to have created a display for the Empress Wu to illustrate this basic principle. He covered an entire hall with mirrors: the floor, walls, and ceiling. In the very center he placed an image of the Buddha, lit with a burning torch next to it. The empress saw the image of the Buddha in the mirrors, but she could also see the mirroring of the mirrored images as infinitely repeating Buddhas. With this powerful experience, she came to understand the meaning of the infinite interpenetration of all things.

This sutra contains another example that was used to explain this paradox, known as Indra's net—a net of precious pearls that hung over Indra's palace. Each of the pearls reflected all the others, so that when you looked at one pearl, all were seen. If you grasped one pearl, you grasped the whole net. Each individual entity is unique while also reflecting and affecting the universe within it. The world of objects is thought of as a series of mirrors reflecting one another, creating an infinity of interactions within their images, so that each includes the others within itself.

Through enlightenment, the practitioner realizes the Oneness of the relationship between objects in the world and emptiness. The universe and all individuals are empty of actual reality. Yet there can be no emptiness without appearances. Even though everything is empty of any reality of an intrinsic individual nature, we have the illusion of *something*. A mirage of water on a hot highway is a real experience, yet it has no intrinsic reality as a "real" object in the world. There is no water on the road.

The inner nature of all phenomena is empty, not merely the outer form or appearance. Since everything shares this same nature, each requires its opposite for its coming into existence. All is in harmony, part of the whole. Existence and nonexistence share the same nature. Oneness is all in this "all in one" philosophy.

● ● ●

The background influences on Zen were broad and pervasive. Zen was to incorporate many of these philosophies, sects, and sutras on its journey around the world, without losing touch with its deeper essence: the enlightenment of the Buddha-mind.

To Be Enlightened: Chinese Ch'an

MANY CREDIT CHINA WITH THE CREATION OF CH'AN, or Zen. The Chinese took India's metaphysical philosophies and transformed them into the distinctive form of Zen Buddhism. The seeds of Zen were brought to China in the fifth century by the legendary Bodhidharma. The growth and development of Zen was nourished by Taoism and Confucianism, two indigenous Chinese philosophies. During the T'ang dynasty (618–907), Zen branched out further, cultivated by generations of charismatic masters. This helped Zen flower in the later Sung periods (960–1279), when it would be transmitted to Japan and then westward.

•

Bodhidharma, The First Chinese Patriarch

I originally came to China,

To transmit the teaching and save deluded beings.

One flower opens five petals,

And the fruit ripens of itself. [1]

Bodhidharma

Bodhidharma (440–528) is recognized by Zen practitioners around the world as the original patriarch of Zen Buddhism. Not only was he the first to introduce Zen to China, but he is also credited with bringing tea and martial arts. Many legends surround this dynamic man, and historians have devoted extensive study to try to authenticate the stories. Most believe that he was a real person, and no one can deny his symbolic importance as the personification of Zen. A few of his sermons have survived the ages; containing the foundation for the Zen spirit, they are still meaningful today. His simple and direct message brought something so unique and special that it has survived for centuries and has found its way around the world.

Bodhidharma came from a Brahmin family in southern India. He was converted to Buddhism at a young age and spent many years studying with Prajnatara, a renowned Buddhist master. Bodhidharma distinguished himself as a serious and talented student. His teacher gave him his religious name, Bodhidharma, "the Law of Enlightenment." It is said that Bodhidharma had a strong personality and dark, penetrating eyes that seemed to see deeply into the very nature of the soul. His teacher, on his deathbed, beseeched Bodhidharma to bring his enlightenment to China. Bodhidharma promised he would and, after his teacher's death, set out alone, determined to make the long and arduous journey from India to China. Some historians believe that Bodhidharma went by boat, but legend has it that he traveled alone over land. As a Buddhist, Bodhidharma did not believe in harming any living creature. He made the dangerous trek without weapons or protection of any kind. He observed animals in their native habitats and carefully watched them hunt and fight. Over the three years that he traveled, Bodhidharma copied the movements of the animals and incorporated them into his own form of unarmed combat. Later, he would teach these techniques to the monks—and thus began the history of the martial arts. Zen and martial arts were one from the beginning. Upon Bodhidharma's arrival on Chinese soil, Zen Buddhism began.

Why did Bodhidharma come from the West?

Bodhidharma was a man of great wisdom whose creative understanding of Buddhism developed into a new, meditative sect. Despite his many years of traditional Buddhist sutra study and ritualized practice, Bodhidharma recognized a simpler way to follow the Path. At a time when Buddhists were arguing about esoteric distinctions between abstract philosophical issues, Bodhidharma's approach was refreshing. He drew some of his teachings from the Lankavatara Sutra but felt that sutra study in itself could not capture the true essence of his new message. He spoke to the common people. Anyone could achieve enlightenment with his concepts, not just an educated elite.

Bodhidharma wandered and taught. Eventually he was given an audience with Emperor Wu of the Liang dynasty (502–57), a devout and generous Buddhist. Their dialogue is famous. The emperor asked Bodhidharma, "Many monasteries have I built, many scriptures have I distributed. Many alms have I given, and I have upheld the faith. Have I acquired merit?"

Bodhidharma, filled with the naive purity of Zen contemplative nothingness, enthusiastically replied, "None."

"In what then does true merit consist?"

He responded with an understanding that is central to Zen: "In the obliteration of matter by absolute knowledge, not by external acts."

Furious with this answer, which negated all his efforts, the emperor banished Bodhidharma from his royal presence in disgrace. Bodhidharma despaired that anyone could ever receive the teachings that he had traveled such a long distance to communicate. He made his way north to Hunan to the Shaolin Monastery, where he turned toward a wall and meditated in silence for nine years. No one could disturb his calm or get his attention, for he felt that no one was worthy.

Bodhidharma became known for his intense way of meditating. Through these nine years his enlightenment deepened and his reputation grew. Many came to learn from the great meditation master, but Bodhidharma remained steadfast in his practice.

Hui-k'o (487–593) was an educated scholar. He studied Taoism in his youth and was well read in the Chinese classics and the philosophical literature of Buddhism. Despite all his years of study, he felt that his accumulation of knowledge was not enough. He heard about Bodhidharma's amazing capacity for intensity of meditation and decided to seek him out in order to resolve his doubts and set his mind at ease. Hui-k'o's entire outlook on life was altered by this dramatic encounter.

Hui-k'o tried to gain an audience with Bodhidharma, who had been meditating at the cave wall for nearly nine years. Day after day, week after week, Hui-k'o came to him and asked to be taught. Bodhidharma sat in stillness, meditating. The weather grew cold, and icy snow and whipping wind beat upon the two solitary figures—one standing, one sitting quietly—day and night. Finally, on a particularly stormy night, Bodhidharma was moved to compassion for this man who had endured so much for so many months. For the first time in nine years, Bodhidharma looked up and spoke. He asked Hui-k'o, "What do you want?"

Bodhidharma sat in stillness, meditating. No one was worthy.

Hui-k'o said, "Please teach me, master."

Bodhidharma answered sadly, "No one is worthy."

Hui-k'o felt deep emotion sweep over him. To show his sincerity, he cut off his own arm and handed it to Bodhidharma. Without a moment's hesitation, Bodhidharma accepted him as his disciple and gave him the name Hui-k'o, designating him as the dharma heir.

Then Hui-k'o said, "I have studied. I have learned all that one should know, and yet my mind is still not at peace. I beg you, teacher, please give me peace."

Bodhidharma answered, "Bring your mind to me, and I will give it peace."

Hui-k'o answered, "I have looked for my mind, but I cannot find it!"

Bodhidharma said, "Then I have given your mind peace."

With these words, Hui-k'o found enlightenment. He received the bowl and robe from Bodhidharma. This gesture was the traditional symbol of direct transmission and made Hui-k'o the Second Patriarch of Zen. The intense commitment required by this new form of Buddhism, Ch'an (Zen in Japanese), is dramatically portrayed by Hui-k'o's story.

Hui-k'o spent many years deepening his insight with questions to his master. Now that he had experienced enlightenment, he wanted to know what method he should use to maintain enlightenment.

Bodhidharma's answer was simple: contemplate mind. This one method dictated all practices. Meditation alone was all that people needed.

Hui-k'o inquired further, uncertain how one method could be used for all practices. Bodhidharma explained that the mind is the root from which all things grow. If you nourish a root, the plant grows. If you cut the root, the plant dies. He urged Hui-k'o to nourish his mind through meditation.

Bodhidharma began to teach the monks at the Shaolin Monastery. He found that they did not understand the wholehearted devotion required for his new style of meditation. To transmit the absolute unity of mind with body and spirit, Bodhidharma combined meditation with the move-

> **Bodhidharma explained that the mind is the root from which all things grow. If you nourish a root, the plant grows. If you cut the root, the plant dies. He urged Hui-k'o to nourish his mind through meditation.**

ments he had learned from the animals. He communicated the intensity and no-mind awareness he had observed in the animal's fights for survival in the forest. Through the fusion of meditation with movement, the monks began to learn Bodhidharma's approach, and entered the Zen Path. Through the ages, Shaolin monks continued to practice martial arts in conjunction with their religious study. The restored Shaolin Monastery became a renowned center for martial arts as well as Zen. Today, the Shaolin Monastery in Hunan is visited by tourists around the world who want to gain a glimpse into these ancient insights.

Bodhidharma's Zen was a radical departure from traditional Buddhism in many ways. He showed his disciples how to find Zen in everyday life, be it in gazing at a cave wall or in the movements of cranes and tigers. His goal—for everyone to see into their own Buddha-nature—was simple and direct. *Buddha* means "awake," "aware." Bodhidharma guided people to wake up, to penetrate through the many layers of beliefs, concepts, and social concerns that we construct with our minds. Only the mind can lead us back to the path of clarity and awareness.

Unlike those Buddhist monks who devoted much of their lives to the study of sutras, Bodhidharma believed that the Zen Path had little use for written traditions. He believed that people who could see into their own nature do not need to read sutras or invoke Buddhas. Accumulation of knowledge is useless and clouds awareness. Doctrines can be helpful only if they direct attention to the mind, as the story of Hui-k'o dramatizes.

Bodhidharma repeatedly emphasized in his sermons that one's own mind is the Buddha. He noticed how often people looked outside themselves for answers: to gods, to holy books, to experts. He warned his students not to waste their time. Just know your own mind, he encouraged, and you can be enlightened.

Over the centuries, Zen monks have continued to spend much of their time on meditation. They commonly learn one or two sutras that they find personally meaningful. Today Zen practitioners chant portions of sutras, such as the Heart Sutra, for inspiration, but devote the majority of their time to meditation.

Bodhidharma was buried at Tinglin Temple on Bear Ear Mountain. Three years later, an official met Bodhidharma, who said he was on his way back to India. He was carrying his staff with a single sandal hanging from it. This report surprised the monks who had been present at Bodhidharma's burial. Hoping to resolve their disbelief, they returned to his tomb and opened it. All they found was a single sandal. Since then, Bodhidharma has often been pictured with his staff and a single sandal dangling from the end.

No one can deny the powerful significance of Bodhidharma and all the legends that surround him. Bodhidharma-style wall gazing continues to this day in many temples, where participants sit facing away from one another, toward the wall. The many stories and legends over the centuries confirm in our minds Bodhidharma's monumental importance to Zen.

•

The Early Zen Patriarchs

Most scholars agree on the identity of the first four Chinese patriarchs following Bodhidharma: Hui-k'o, Seng-ts'an (d. 606), Tao-hsin (580–651), and Hung-jen (601–74). These dynamic individuals nurtured the seeds for the Zen Buddhism that flourished and grew into a large and influential sect during the T'ang and Sung dynasties.

Hui-k'o stayed with his master for nine years. The religious climate began to change in China during the last quarter of the sixth century. The warm, welcoming atmosphere that had nurtured Buddhism became cold and filled with enmity. Chinese authorities who favored Taoism and Confucianism burned sutras and images of Buddha in an effort to obtain royal patronage. Monks and nuns were forced to return to lay life. Not only did Hui-k'o suffer from general Buddhist persecution in 574, but he also was faced with severe criticism from traditional Buddhist sects. Hui-k'o fled to the mountains, where he hid for many years in obscurity with a few faithful students. Not until he was quite elderly did he feel that it was safe to live in the city where he spent his last ten years teaching. Hui-k'o carried on Bodhidharma's method of wall gazing. He taught his disciples by emphasizing intuitive insight, not sutras and rituals.

Seng-ts'an, faithful student of Hui-k'o, became the Third Patriarch. He was known for his friendliness and gentle, kindly personality. He lived a typical wandering monk's life, homeless and without possessions, fleeing with Hui-k'o to escape the Buddhist persecution. After his master's death,

Hui-k'o taught his disciples by emphasizing intuitive insight, not sutras and rituals.

Seng-ts'an continued to wander all over the country, carefully avoiding the Chinese authorities.

Seng-ts'an is credited with having written the first Zen poem, entitled "Inscribed on the Believing Mind." It is likely that Seng-ts'an wrote down the "Hsinhsinming" to save the teachings of Zen from extinction. The poem, expressing the union of opposites in emptiness, shows how early Taoism blended with Zen as the new sect began to take root in Chinese soil. In this beautiful, simply written poem, the Chinese spirit joins with Buddhist spirituality in celebration of the mysterious Buddha-mind. The literal translation of the title, *hsin* (faith), *hsin* (mind), *ming* (record), encourages all to have faith in the Buddha-mind. The poem leads the listener to rise above the duality of yin and yang to a level where conflict no longer exists: Buddha-mind, empty mind, peaceful and complete. Here are passages from the opening and final lines of this poem:

There is nothing difficult about the Great Way,

But avoid choosing!

Only when you neither love nor hate,

Does it appear in all clarity.

There is no need to worry about perfect knowledge.

The believing mind is not dual;

What is dual is not the believing mind.

Beyond all language,

For it there is no past, no present, no future. [2]

Tao-hsin (580–651), the Fourth Patriarch, made distinct changes in the lifestyle of Zen monks. The previous three patriarchs had been largely itinerant, traveling to various established Buddhist monasteries or hiding in remote areas to escape persecution. They spent their time lecturing, begging, and meditating. Their disciples were few but always intensely devoted to Zen.

Tao-hsin settled on Mount Shuan-feng, where he founded the first Zen community. His dynamic personality drew more than five hundred disciples. There was still no state support for Zen at this time, and begging could not bring in enough to sustain the large group of monks who wanted to study under Tao-hsin. In response to these circumstances, he set up a monastic community in which all the monks shared in household tasks as well as farming. He believed that going, standing, sitting, lying down—all are Zen. Here began the Zen tradition of maintaining the inner spirit of Zen throughout a day of meditation along with work. The community was able to survive, independent of any outside assistance.

Tao-hsin altered forever the Zen monk's life. No longer wandering beggars, Zen monks established monastic traditions of their own. Living your Zen in every minute of your life through daily routines can be said to have begun with Tao-hsin.

Hung-jen (601–74), the Fifth Patriarch and Tao-hsin's successor, began his lifetime of devotion at age six. His intensity was legendary. He worked all day and then meditated all night until dawn. After he was given the symbolic robe and bowl, he moved to Mount P'ing-jung, now remembered as the Mountain of the Fifth Patriarch. He continued to follow the monastic lifestyle initiated by his teacher, Tao-hsin.

Little is known about Hung-jen himself, but he is remembered for the many great disciples he taught. After he certified that his students had found enlightenment, he encouraged them to travel and start their own monasteries. At least five different lines of Zen attribute their roots to Hung-jen, each branching off with their own variations. Hung-jen helped Zen thrive and be more diverse. Unfortunately, this policy also led to difficulties.

•

The Two Sixth Patriarchs:
A Period of Conflict and Renewal

Controversy surrounds the next period of Zen. Hung-jen had many students, but two of his protégés distinguished themselves as exceptional: Shen-hsiu and Hui-neng. Two opposing Zen stories arose, one claiming that Shen-hsiu was the Sixth Patriarch and the other stating that Hui-neng was the true dharma heir. This created a great split between the two ideologically different schools; they came to be known as the Northern and Southern Schools. The difference in Zen styles was the essence of this struggle. History reveals that the argument between the Northern and Southern Schools was initiated by the disciples of the two Sixth Patriarchs after their deaths. We present both stories to you because each portrays an aspect of the Zen spirit that lives on today.

Shen-hsiu: Northern School

Shen-hsiu (605–706) joined Hung-jen's monastic community on the East Mountain at the age of fifty. He was well educated in the Chinese classics, Taoism, and Confucianism and quickly rose to be first among the disciples. When Hung-jen was ready to retire, he presented Shen-hsiu with the traditional robe and the bowl to carry forth the teachings as the Sixth Patriarch. After Shen-hsiu received the Dharma Seal, he left the East Mountain to deepen his understanding in solitary meditation. He returned to the provincial capitals of Loyang and Ch'ang-an and used the Yü-ch'uan-ssu Monastery as his base. Shen-hsiu was held in very high esteem and gained many honors. By a.d. 730, Ch'an Buddhism was firmly established, with its own lineage from Bodhidharma to Shen-hsiu, recognition by the royal court and high officials, and wide acceptance from the populace, both educated and uneducated. Over his many years as a monk (he reputedly lived more than one hundred years), Shen-hsiu did much to spread and popularize the practice of Zen.

Shen-hsiu was a traditionalist, following the heritage of the Lankavatara Sutra and the preceding patriarchs. He taught his students to calm the mind through devotion to meditation. From the calm mind (samadhi) arose an undisturbed state of perfect wisdom (prajna). He believed that when people clear the mind completely, an enlightened state shines through. Shen-hsiu taught that enlightenment comes gradually, through diligent, sincere, disciplined practice over time. This became known as the method of gradual cultivation.

Shen-hsiu passed along the leadership of his school to P'u-chi (651–739), who became the Seventh Patriarch. The Northern Zen School of Shen-hsiu and P'u-chi was at first the accepted, mainstream form of Zen in China.

Bitter conflict with the Southern School and perceived limits in Shen-hsiu's approach brought about the dissipation and eventual disappearance of the Northern School. Despite the end of the Northern School, certain of its qualities— quiet mind and the method of gradual cultivation—were integrated into later sects to become part of the Zen spirit today.

Hui-neng: Southern School

Hui-neng (638–713) began the Southern School of Zen. He claimed to be the true Sixth Patriarch, which is expressed and argued in detail in the famous work, the Platform Sutra.

Hui-neng came from a poor family. He made a humble living selling firewood to support his widowed mother. During one of his deliveries, he heard the Diamond Sutra being recited. As he listened to the words, the illiterate firewood peddler was struck with a sudden experience: enlightenment. This was to became the cornerstone of his Southern School, that true Zen enlightenment comes in a flash, not through years and years of gradual development. Following his realization, Hui-neng arranged for his mother's care and set out on the three-month journey by foot to reach the famous Zen monastery on East Mountain. He spoke to the master when he arrived, and even though Hui-neng was a layman, Hung-jen recognized his potential and gave him a place to sleep and work to do as a rice pounder.

Hung-jen grew older and realized that it was time to pass on the leadership to the next generation. He gathered all his disciples together and told them to seek an experience of enlightenment and then write a poem about it. Whoever showed the highest understanding with his poem would be given the robe and the Dharma Seal, to become the Sixth Patriarch.

Shen-hsiu, who was the number-one disciple of the monastery, wrote his poem on a wall where the master would certainly see it. This was what he wrote:

Our body is the bodhi tree

And our mind a mirror bright.

Carefully we wipe them now by hour

And let no dust alight. [3]

The master knew immediately upon reading it that Shen-hsiu had not yet found enlightenment. Hui-neng heard the poem being recited while he was pounding rice. He also recognized that the composer had not yet realized essence of mind. This motivated Hui-neng to compose his own poem. Because Hui-neng was illiterate, a young boy who was passing by wrote it down for him. Hui-neng's stanza read as follows:

There is no bodhi-tree

Nor stand of a mirror bright.

Since all is void,

Where can the dust alight? [4]

The Fifth Patriarch realized that Hui-neng had a deep understanding, but he did not wish to tell his disciples, since Hui-neng was only a layman. At midnight, Hung-jen met with Hui-neng privately, transmitted to him the Dharma of Sudden Enlightenment, and gave him the robe of succession. However, since Hui-neng was not the recognized number-one student, the master sent him away. Obediently, Hui-neng set out with the robe and the dharma, never to return to the monastery. The story ends with Hui-neng's departure southward.

Hui-neng's ideas were different from those of Northern Zen but still remained within the Buddhist tradition. Hui-neng distinguished himself from Shen-hsiu by holding that there should be no separation between mind and enlightenment: they are one. Meditation and wisdom are one, like the lamp and the light it gives forth. Thus, to purify the mind in order to let enlightenment shine through implied that the mind was not identical with enlightenment, but merely its vehicle. The Buddha-mind in us all is already pure. The "dust wiping Zen," as Hui-neng called the Northern School's approach, took a superficial and incorrect path to enlightenment. There is no form, no substance. Hui-neng denied the value of gradual cultivation.

Hui-neng held that mind and enlightenment are one.

Hui-neng's method of meditation dispensed with all formalities. No exact instructions were given. He rejected the use of meditative postures, so that the mind could be free to circulate. "No clinging, no attachment" applied to meditative practices as well. All that mattered was practicing with a wholehearted, straightforward attitude. When people do so sincerely, they will suddenly experience their original mind. The original mind is also called self-nature, Buddha-nature, reality, and purity. What all these names refer to, when experienced directly, constitutes enlightenment. This was Hui-neng's optimistic approach.

Unlike the Northern School, Hui-neng encouraged his followers not to dwell on emptiness of consciousness. Emptiness includes everything: earth, mountains, good people, bad people, "the ten thousand things." As you observe this, do not cling to it, but do not disregard it either. This is what he meant when he taught his students to be apart from birth and death.

Hui-neng's method made sense to the common person. Coming from such a humble background himself, he could say confidently to his followers, "I was awakened to *satori* suddenly, and you can be, too." He believed that all humanity is equal in the dharma. He encouraged people to seek out teachers and even read the sutras, especially the Diamond Sutra, if they felt they must. But he strongly cautioned that you cannot find enlightenment outside your own mind. A good teacher can guide you in the right direction, but ultimately the answer is within your own mind.

Ho-tse Shen-hui (670–762), not to be confused with Shen-hsiu, was Hui-neng's disciple. Shen-hui became the Seventh Patriarch. Intent on building a new school of his own, Shen-hui probably did more to launch the Southern School's dominance and derail the Northern School's popularity than anyone else. Succeeding generations of Zen masters have attributed their lineage to Hui-neng and the Sudden Enlightenment School. However, many of the teachings from the Northern School—of continuous, calm, meditation practice, with no concern for sudden enlightenment—can be seen today in the Soto School of Zen.

The Zen ancestors:
Bodhidharma
Hui-k'o
Seng-ts'an
Tao-hsin
Hung-jen
Hui-neng

•

The T'ang Dynasty Period (618–907): The Golden Age of Zen

The disciples of Hui-neng's Sudden Enlightenment School spread the new Zen message. Radically innovative to the extreme, these Zen monks boldly burned images and sutras, laughed, shouted, and even struck one another in order to teach Zen. They feared nothing and communed with their unconscious minds. Living in a state of heightened spirituality, they experienced unimaginable and absolute freedom.

During the T'ang period, the mysterious Tao merged with the unfathomable Buddha-mind. Anti-intellectualism was proclaimed to be the way to find true wisdom. Just as in Taoism, where not-knowing is the path to wisdom, so the Zen monks believed that knowledge is illusion. If you really understand the Tao, you understand the vast, boundless void beyond all right and wrong, good and bad. Zen monks did not rely on sutras, just as the Taoist sage abhors the accumulation of knowledge. Taoist wisdom and Buddhist enlightenment are one.

The Zen philosopher-scholars of the period altered the concept of the Tao of Taoism to fit their Buddhist paradigm. Instead of being an abstract absolute as it is in Taoism, the Zen concept of Tao belonged to the everyday mind at work in everyday life. Zen was to be for the common person.

Taoist wisdom and Buddhist enlightenment are one.

The Zen masters who are remembered (among the many who have been lost in the annals of time) gave Zen its uniquely Chinese individualistic spirit. Three generations after Hui-neng, two great masters emerged: Ma-tsu and Shih-t'ou. Both men's exuberance and spontaneity gave a new intensity to Zen. Many talented disciples passed through their gates, stirring up a spiritual storm that has left an indelible mark in history.

The Lines of Ma-tsu and Shih-t'ou

Ma-tsu: The Great Solitary One

Ma-tsu (709–88) believed ardently in sudden enlightenment. Ma-tsu could be forceful, direct, and even rude. According to legend, he had the stride of a bull and the gaze of a tiger.

He was the first Zen monk known to use shouting and shock to foster enlightenment. His bizarre tactics brought about experiential gaps in the minds of his disciples, causing momentary states of confusion. The next step often led to enlightenment. A particularly paradoxical exchange between Ma-tsu and his famous student Pai-chang has been recorded as a koan. Just as Pai-chang found himself thoroughly confused, Ma-tsu grabbed his nose and twisted it until Pai-chang yelled out in pain. At that moment, the disciple experienced enlightenment.

Ma-tsu, like Hui-neng before him, believed that everything is mind. But always he expressed this paradoxically. "This is not mind, this is not Buddha, this is not a thing." [5]

Ma-tsu is remembered in the *Hekiganroku* for the enigmatic words "Sun-faced Buddha, Moon-faced Buddha" that he uttered just before he died. The words refer indirectly to a passage in a sutra that makes the point that whether one's life is short or long, the Buddha's lifetime is timeless.

A monk said to Hōgen, "My name is Echō. I ask you, what is the Buddha?" Hōgen said, "You are Echō."
—from the *Hekiganroku*

Shih-t'ou: Stone Head

Shih-t'ou (700–790) stood in Hui-neng's direct lineage. As a young student, he distinguished himself beyond all others. His teacher said, "I have many horned cattle, but one unicorn is enough." [6] Shih-t'ou was given the Dharma Seal and took up residence in Hunan province. He built himself a tiny hut on top of a wide, flat rock, from which he received his nickname, Stone Head. He remained in meditative seclusion for twenty-three years. Shih-t'ou's quiet, penetrating thinking attracted the attention of many disciples, who flocked to study with him. Eventually his disciples persuaded him to open a monastery.

Disciples streamed to study with both Ma-tsu and Shih-t'ou. Their Zen challenged conscious limits, bringing students to recognize the wisdom of their unconscious minds. The T'ang monks who followed carried on the creative and often baffling traditions.

The Zen masters pushed paradox and incongruity to

the limits, thereby bringing about enlightenment. Chao-chou Ts'ung-shen (778–897), a descendant of Ma-tsu, when asked for instructions to reach enlightenment, answered, "Wash your bowls." This master was to inspire modern Korean Zen.

These novel, seemingly erratic techniques bewildered and perplexed the disciples. The comforts of certainty were broken. Minds opened to nonrational possibilities. "When your mind is without anything, you are no-mind, then you are free and spiritual, empty and marvelous." [7]

Pai-chang: Working with Enlightenment

The T'ang period monk Pai-chang (720–824) defined the monastic lifestyle that was later brought to both Japan and Korea. During the early years of Zen, monks lived as part of larger Buddhist temples, quietly practicing in small Zen communities. Following the tradition of Tao-hsin (Fourth Patriarch), Pai-chang set up a purely Zen monastery with its own clear-cut rules for Zen monastic life. This freed Zen from other Buddhist sects and also gave the monks autonomy from the social order in general.

Pai-chang defined the monastic lifestyle.

Like all Buddhists, the Zen monks took on moral injunctions against unethical behavior: no killing, stealing, lying, or drinking alcohol. They also swore to take on a life of poverty and chastity. Each monk had only a straw mat for eating and sleeping. Everyone worked in the Zen monastery: "A day without work is a day without eating," Pai-chang often told his disciples. One time, when Pai-chang was very old and somewhat ill, his monks tried to take away his garden tools to spare him from work. Rather than feeling grateful, Pai-chang refused to eat until they returned the tools and let him labor in the garden. Daily life in the monastery always included work as well as meditation.

Through these rules, regulations, and customs, to be followed daily, Pai-chang passed along a lasting system that was easy to follow, with less likelihood for corruption. This system was learned by the Korean monks who journeyed to learn at Pai-chang's monastery. They returned to their own mountain temples and put the routines into practice. Many Zen monasteries thrived throughout China as separate and independent institutions. This independence allowed Zen to escape the drastic persecution of Buddhism that took place in China between the years 841 and 845. Most Buddhist sects were completely obliterated, but Zen escaped largely untouched, and therefore flourished.

Huang-po: To Know Is Not to Know

Huang-po (d. 850) was the monk who taught Lin-chi—founder of the Rinzai School—and therefore is given an important place in Zen history. He was a focused, inspirational teacher with thousands of students flocking to his monastery at Vulture Peak on Mount Huang-po. He was given the dharma name of Huang-po for the mountain where he taught, as was the custom.

Huang-po repeatedly expressed to his students that they must give up all conceptual thinking. "All the concepts you have formed in the past must be discarded and replaced by Void." [8]

Huang-po was against learning from books, scriptures, or doctrines of any kind—even Buddhist ones. Over and over he urged his students to halt such concept-forming activities. Then and only then could they transcend the bonds of knowledge.

He took this to the most radical conclusion possible when he said, "The Way of the Buddhas and the Way of the devils are equally wide of the mark." [9]

The true Way was beyond all dualities and distinctions. He believed that there is no square and round, no right and wrong, no hatred or love, no victory or defeat. "All wisdom and all holiness are but streaks of lightning." [10]

Huang-po believed in direct transmission, mind to mind.

Huang-po believed in direct transmission, mind to mind. Without the use of words, this communication was almost telepathic. The dharma that he passed along to Lin-chi communicated pure essence of mind. Lin-chi would carry this forth, devising creative teaching methods that brought about a rebirth of the Zen spirit.

When Huang-po died, the Emperor Hsuan Tsung gave him the title "The Zen Master Who Destroys All Limitations," a name well suited to this devoted and sincere Zen master.

• • •

Ma-tsu's line exemplified four generations of direct transmission at its best, from Ma-tsu to Pai-chang to Huang-po to Lin-chi, who was the originator of the famous Rinzai School and has been remembered as one of the greatest Zen masters of all times.

Lin-chi: The Shout of Enlightenment

Lin-chi (d. 866) made lasting contributions to Zen, taking it to a new level of clarity and universality. Zen owes a great debt to the main compiler of Lin-chi's many teachings, Li Tsun-hzu (d. 1038), a lay disciple of the Lin-chi School. Thanks to his writings, the Lin-chi School grew vigorously during this period.

Lin-chi's enlightenment experience came from the combined teachings of two monks, his master Huang-po (d. 850), and the hermit monk Ta-yu (d. c. 850), a disciple of Ma-tsu. After his enlightenment, Lin-chi settled in northern China at a tiny monastery next to the Hu-t'o River. The monastery was called Lin-chi (in Japanese, Rinzai-in), meaning "monastery overlooking the ford." Based in the perspicacity of Lin-chi, the Rinzai School would grow over the centuries to become one of the most influential Zen schools in the world.

In many ways, Lin-chi's message embodies much of the American spirit. He proclaimed that the ordinary person is fully capable of enlightenment in an instantaneous flash, just by being fully and authentically oneself. Lin-chi accepted the Mahayana Buddhist belief that the Buddha-mind is within everyone, but he went further. The genuine, wise human exists here and now in you and me. Stop trying to talk about it or practice to reach it: be enlightened now! Nothing is missing. You are the buddha patriarch just as you are. His words to his monks are just as relevant to us today as they were then:

Lin-chi proclaimed that the ordinary person is capable of enlightenment.

When students today fail to make progress, where's the fault? The fault lies in the fact that they don't have faith in themselves! If you don't have faith in yourself, then you'll be forever in a hurry trying to keep up with everything around you, you'll be twisted and turned by whatever environment you're in and you can never move freely. But if you can just stop this mind that goes rushing around moment by moment looking for something, then you'll be no different from the patriarchs and buddhas. [11]

The only thing keeping people from truth is their own selves, mistakenly seeking support from sources other than their inner true wise nature. This takes the original conception of Buddha-mind from Bodhidharma even further. The true human of no rank—that is, anyone—depends on nothing external.

Lin-chi's faith and confidence in the natural inner person drew from Taoism. People should have vitality, be free-wheeling and unpredictable. In fact, Lin-chi's teaching methods were wildly unpredictable. He might shout loudly or hit with his stick until the student experienced pain. These shocking tactics were intended to bring about sudden enlightenment in a manner similar to the way he had experienced it with his own teacher.

Lin-chi also incorporated Taoism when he presented his lessons as opposites, like yin and yang. For example, he might say, "There is no dharma outside, but don't look inside." The lesson did not stop there, for he moved his students toward a dialectical synthesis, beyond either opposite, pushing them toward higher consciousness. After his death, the Lin-chi School drew from these lessons to present students with structured dialectics to help them reach enlightenment.

Here is a typical exchange between Lin-chi and one of his students:

> A monk asked, "What is the basic meaning of Buddhism?"
> The Master held his fly wisk straight up.
> The monk gave a shout.
> The Master struck him. [12]

Lin-chi was an exceptional person. Through his loud yell and sharp blows, he knocked sense into his students, to firmly plant Zen timelessly in the here and now. He is remembered, even revered, by Rinzai descendants. His methods and focus have continued, growing stronger with later generations, eventually becoming one of the two most widespread schools of Zen around the world! Yet his views were to be considerably modified, balanced with other philosophies (such as Confucianism and Taoism), as they were incorporated into modern Rinzai Zen.

•

The Five Houses

During the second half of the T'ang dynasty, the spirit of the T'ang masters evolved. Zen began to separate into different styles, or houses. Each house had its own emphasis on methods and practices, yet underlying them all was the cohesive Zen spirit. The five houses were the Lin-chi School, the

Ts'ao-tung School (later to be known as Soto), the Kuei-yang School, the Yun-men School, and the Fa-yen School. Two of these houses were to survive, incorporating the best from all the schools as their teachings were brought to Japan and on to the West: Rinzai and Soto.

Lin-chi School: Rinzai

The Rinzai School grew during the Sung period (960–1279) to usher in a whole new phase of Zen. As Zen developed after the creative T'ang period, it became more codified and structured. Rinzai tried to remain true to Lin-chi's many innovations, such as abrupt shouting and striking students with a stick. Later Rinzai masters preserved Lin-chi's techniques within a teachable system without sacrificing their founder's unique character. They classified their master's techniques with analogies instead of direct concepts. For example, they formulated four types of shouting derived from Lin-chi's methods, considered characteristic of the approach of his lineage:

> Sometimes a shout is like the jeweled sword of the Vajra King; sometimes a shout is like the golden-haired lion crouching on the ground; sometimes a shout is like a weed-tipped fishing pole; sometimes a shout doesn't function as a shout. [13]

The later masters also found a deeper metaphysical quality implicit in Lin-chi's simple, direct methods. The *Discourses on the Record of Lin-chi* elaborated on the master's teachings about being and nonbeing. There were other formulas as well, such as "The Three Statements," "The Three Mysteries," and "The Three Essences." Even though these monks felt that such formulas were helpful adjuncts to practice, the essence of the house remained in the concrete realization of immediate experience. These formulations helped later generations continue to incorporate the creativity of the T'ang masters. Gradually, however, their spontaneity gave way to the more structured and stylized koan practice and moral philosophy popular in the Sung period.

Ts'ao-tung School: Soto

The second major school that would later become a worldwide phenomenon was the Ts'ao-tung School, known more widely by its Japanese name, Soto. It takes its name from combining the names of the mountains near the monasteries, also adopted as dharma names by the two founders, Tung-shan Liang-chieh (807–69) and his disciple, Ts'ao-shan Pen-chi (840–901).

Tung-shan learned under a student of Ma-tsu. Once he asked his teacher, "Can you draw a portrait of your master a hundred years from now?" His master replied, "Just this is it." Tung-shan did not understand this answer, so he left to wander through the woods. As he was crossing a stream, he saw his face reflected in the water. In a flash he understood what his teacher had been trying to communicate to him: enlightenment must be completely one's own.

Ts'ao-shan developed the insights of Tung-shan even further. He was somewhat different from the other monks because he loved to study. He spent many years in quiet contemplation, but through the depth of his understandings, he was able to penetrate the meaning of the Five Ranks and pass this along to disciples. The Five Ranks of the House of Ts'ao-tung are so important to Zen that Hakuin, an eighteenth-century Japanese Rinzai Zen master, said it was the essential path to Zen practice.

The formula of the Five Ranks is an attempt to give a step-by-step pathway to enlightenment. Originating long ago in the Indian Mahayana metaphysics, the Five Ranks were given a Chinese flavor through the work of T'ang master Shih-t'ou, a contemporary of Ma-tsu.

The main concept of the Five Ranks addresses the meaning and the relationship between the apparent and the real, relative and absolute reality, fact and principle. Duality itself is explored as the practitioner evolves toward enlightenment.

The Five Ranks theory is based on the belief that there is no fundamental difference between the insights arrived at through Zen meditation and the insights attained by Mahayana Buddhist scholars through philosophical questions and study. Many of these same questions have been posed by Western philosophy and modern science (theory and application, being and nonbeing, fact and essence, to name a few). The theory is obscure and paradoxical to the conscious mind, but is revealed through meditation.

The First Rank probes the *apparent within the real.* The beam of enlightenment's spotlight shines on reality, revealing darkness. Nothing exists. Reality is a hollow shell. At the Second Rank, *the real within the apparent,* the world is turned inside out. With the realization of nonexistence, all seems empty, devoid of substance. Nonbeing seems more real than being. As one might imagine, this can lead to passivity, and until this level is transcended, meditators might become apathetic, unmotivated, lost in meaningless nonbeing. Yet the Third Rank, *coming from within the real* beckons: oneness with the world. Meditators begin to understand that things interrelate with one another. The everyday world and the meditator's mind fuse into one. This is followed by the Fourth Rank, *mutual integration,* with a feeling of compassion for all beings, through which meditators seek to reach out to help them. In this rank, meditators can act within the everyday world, yet not be drawn by the seductive lure of defilements and materialism's quicksand. Even this must be transcended to the Fifth Rank, *unity attained.* Enlightened meditators now live without hesitation, fully in the world yet not quite of the world.

Ts'ao-shan also drew diagrams illustrating the Five Ranks using circles, black and white. Zen practitioners used these drawings as a guide to practice, a visual aid to map the shift from the everyday world of phenomena to the unified nondualistic world of enlightenment.

Kuei-yang School

The Kuei-yang School of "experience through action" was begun by two monks, one of whom was a student of Pai-chang. The enlightenment experience of Kuei-shan Liang-yu (771–853) set the tone for the school's development.

Pai-chang set a large jug of water at the foot of his disciple. He looked at him knowingly and demanded, "If you can't call this a water jug, what do you call it?" Kuei-shan answered with a wordless gesture by kicking the jug over and walking away. Pai-chang knew by this that his disciple had found enlightenment.

Zen enlightenment is beyond words, so the monks of this school used action and silence to express it. "Swordplay," as they called it, helped many find their experience of enlightenment. These kinds of exchanges later became known as "dharma combat."

The Zen insight is beyond all learning from books.

Students felt confused when presented with these sorts of questions at the Kuei-yang School. But if a disciple asked for an explanation of these baffling dilemmas, the master might answer, "You cannot fill an empty stomach with paintings of rice cakes." The Zen insight is beyond all learning from books, even the classics. It may come in a wordless moment, from a sudden sound, or even in profound silence.

Yun-men School

This house developed from the line of Shih-t'ou, a contemporary of Ma-tsu. Yun-men Wen-yen (864–949) was known for his short, sharp answers to questions: "one-word barriers." When asked, "What is the way?" he answered, "Grab it." Once a monk asked him about a sword so sharp that it could cut a hair blown across its blade. Yun-men's reply: "Bones." Yun-men's incisive statements helped his students to step outside conscious reason to find an enlightened mind.

The House of Yun-men continued into the Sung dynasty period, influencing the upper classes through its cultured use of poetry. Hsueh-tou Ch'ung-hsein (980–1052), one of the students of Yun-men's successor (Chih-men Kuang-tsu, d. 1031), expressed his Zen through poetry, as had his teacher. Hsueh-tou Ch'ung-hsein was the author of the one hundred verses of the *Hekiganroku,* which was to become a beacon, guiding later Zen seekers toward enlightenment. He attempted to epitomize poetically the essence of Zen's teachings through the wisdom of the masters. He used eighteen cases from Yun-men, immortalizing the "one-word barriers" of the House of Yun-men long after the school was gone.

Fa-yen School

The House of Fa-yen, located in southern China, drew many disciples to hear the wisdom of its founder, Fa-yen (885–958). His approach to Zen was gentler than some of the others. He never hit or shouted. Rather, he used a subtler method to guide his students to enlightenment. One of his favorite techniques was to answer a question by repeating the question as a statement. His insight into living Zen is reflected in this typical response to the question "What should a Zen monk do throughout the day and night?" The answer: "Every step should tread on this question." [14]

•

Sung Dynasty Period (960–1279):
Cultural Flowering

The Sung emperors wielded less political power than previous dynasties; nonetheless, in the tenth through the thirteenth centuries, Chinese culture experienced a renaissance.

People again studied the ancient Chinese classics of Taoism and Confucianism. New philosophical interpretations were given. Theories that improved each of the philosophies by integrating their concepts soon dominated the intellectual, cultural, and political life.

Buddhism played a lesser role than it had before, never fully recovering from the great persecution of 845. The only sects of Buddhism that survived were Zen and Pure Land. Zen monks, who had always considered themselves Buddhists, felt an obligation to keep the Buddhist heritage alive. In order to do so, they turned to the written word, moved to the cities, and even involved themselves in the politics of the day. Previously, Zen monks had not been involved in the imperial court but instead had lived independently in small, rural temples. During the Sung dynasty, this changed. With the widespread practice of Zen, the imperial court established lavish Zen temples near the cities. Ta-hui Tsung-kao (1089–1163) and his Rinzai master Yuan-wu moved to the city and found themselves involved in court life. The move was not without sacrifice, for although the Zen masters of the Sung period may have been given impressive temples and court favor, they gave up the absolute freedom enjoyed by the T'ang masters. By the time of the Southern Sung dynasty, a state temple system (known as Five Mountains, Ten Temples) graded practitioners and put them through a fixed curriculum. Great numbers of people trained in Zen practice during the Sung dynasty, making it a productive period. The Five Mountains, Ten Temples system was brought to Japan and used to spread Rinzai Zen. The Five Houses of Zen gradually consolidated into two major lines: Soto, under Hung-chih Cheng-chueh (1091–1157), and Rinzai, under Ta-hui. Rinzai received the most recognition from the government. Although Hung-chih and Ta-hui had been friends, they disputed back and forth on Zen practice. Ta-hui rejected all sitting in meditation. He attacked the custom of sitting still, criticizing silent meditation for being as lifeless as "cold ashes or a withered tree." He believed that koan practice put students into a useful state of great doubt; enlightenment arises from the intense search that evolves from this doubt. By contrast, Hung-chih accused the Rinzai School of koan-gazing. He believed that silent illumination derives from the authentic tradition of Bodhidharma, that silence forms the basis for an enlightened mind through stillness.

Rinzai and Soto were both strong traditions with clear-cut methods to use. Both sects would be carried to Korea and Japan, where they would experience new creative impetus.

The Koan

The greatest innovation of the Sung period was the use of the *kung-an,* the *koan.* Koans present a puzzle or question for students to solve. The answer requires an alteration of consciousness that lies outside logical, rational thought. The Sung dynasty masters, now upstanding members of Chinese society, were more restricted in their behavior than the nonconforming, unpredictable T'ang masters. However, they captured the inspirational qualities of their predecessors through the use of koans. The first monk to use koans was Rinzai master Nan-yuan Hui-yung (d. 930). He confronted his disciples with the same words the T'ang masters had used with their own students: seemingly irrational non sequiturs that altered consciousness. In time, many Sung masters successfully incorporated koans into their teaching. They found that groups of disciples could be presented with the same koan. If the students put themselves wholeheartedly into the effort of solving the koan, they would reach enlightenment.

> What the koan proposes to do is to develop artificially or systematically in the consciousness of the Zen followers what the early masters produced in themselves spontaneously. It also aspires to develop the Zen experience in a greater number of minds than the masters could otherwise hope for. [15]

D. T. Suzuki's view is that even though koans mechanized Zen somewhat, they also saved it from oblivion. The wildly creative and spontaneous spirit of T'ang period Zen could grow and evolve despite the structures of organized court religion.

Eventually, these koans were collected into books. The earliest koan collection to be systematically presented in three volumes was called *Fun'yoroku* in Japanese (*Fen-yang-lu* in Chinese), written by Fen-yang (947–1024). He rewrote some of the paradoxical, provocative statements in the *Rinzairoku* and recorded the many early stories he had heard. Other koan books by Rinzai masters helped launch Rinzai as the most powerful school in China. There were over seventeen hundred Chinese koans. The innovation of the koan has helped the Zen spirit travel across time and space to reach us today.

Two koan collections have lived on into the twentieth

century, the *Hekiganroku* (*Blue Cliff Record*) and the *Mumonkan* (*Gateless Gate*). Both have been translated into English by several different people. [16]

The *Hekiganroku* koans were originally collected by the poet-monk Hsueh-tou Ch'ung-hsien (980–1052), a member of the House of Yun-men, which eventually was absorbed into the Lin-chi line. Yuan-wu K'o-ch'in (1063–1105), who came from a family of Confucian scholars, added clear commentaries and notes on each koan. The collection became a complex work with theoretical value, making it an even more useful teaching tool.

The *Hekiganroku*, with its stories, verses, and commentaries, was written clearly—so clearly that Yuan-wu's successor, Ta-hui, burned almost every copy, along with the printer's blocks. Some think he did it because he believed that such an explicit book would interfere with the necessary struggle with doubt that one must endure to find true enlightenment. Instead of using this collection, Ta-hui popularized a technique of asking questions, called Hua-t'ou, to lure the student to a mental precipice: the boundary of effective use of problem-solving thought. This technique was brought to Korea by Korean monks to be developed further and used in Korean Zen. The *Hekiganroku* disappeared for two hundred years until a lay Buddhist, Chang Ming-yuan, gathered all the available copies and created a new edition in 1300.

The *Mumonkan,* a collection of forty-eight cases of enlightenment of Buddha and the patriarchs, was considered a primary koan collection. It is blunt in its attempt to speak to the unconscious mind. Each entry includes a title, the koan, and a critical commentary by the compiler, Master Wu-men Hui-k'ai (1183–1260)—Mumon—a Rinzai monk. He explains his choice of title: No-gate is the gate of emancipation. No-mind is the mind of Tao. This book has been central in Japanese Zen.

•

Ming Dynasty Period (1368–1644): Unification of All Buddhism

Once Zen became involved in society, it opened itself to outside influences. Gradually, the Pure Land sect mixed with Zen. Some monks combined meditation with repetition of the holy name of Amitabha. Soto was absorbed into Rinzai in China, forging all Zen into one sect. A syncretistic movement unified all Buddhist sects with Confucianism and Taoism.

A syncretistic movement unified all Buddhist sects with Confucianism and Taoism.

Although Zen did not have an entirely separate identity in China, there were individuals who continued to carry on the Zen traditions. One example was Yin-yuan Lung-ch'i (Ingen-Ryuki, 1592–1673), a student of the Lin-chi School, who emigrated to Japan (1654) with artisans to found the Obaku sect in Japan. The Japanese emperor gave him land, and he built a monastery and temple in the Ming style at Uji, near Kyoto.

As Zen moved to other countries, such as Japan, those monks who remained in China contributed to the unification. The Japanese monks who came to China searching for the dharma brought their enlightenment experiences back to their native Japan, helping Zen to be reborn anew as the spirit of Zen moved onward.

TO DO *and to* BE ENLIGHTENED ARE ONE: JAPANESE ZEN

BUDDHISM WAS FIRST INTRODUCED IN JAPAN through a precious artifact from Korea during the sixth century. Zen did not take hold until much later when, in the latter part of the twelfth century, a Japanese monk known as Eisai traveled to China, to the source of T'ien-t'ai (Tendai) Buddhism. He returned a second time, found enlightenment in Rinzai Zen, and brought it back to Japan. He has been granted the honor of being called the founder of the Rinzai sect of Zen in Japan. Rinzai Zen teaches that one can continue to evolve by contemplating appropriate koans through the microscope of meditation. Enlightenment can be deepened and enlarged as it is guided through a curriculum of sophisticated philosophical experiences, resulting in a reorientation of the mind.

Soto Zen followed from the pilgrimage of Dogen, a student of Eisai's successor, whose dream was to gain the true dharma through study with Zen teachers in China. There, he found a master who gave him the direction his life was to follow.

Dogen came to believe that continued practice of stilling the mind in meditation is the primary path to enlightenment.

Numerous applications have enriched Zen, initiated by the ingenuity of the Japanese people. Disciplines such as swordsmanship, teaism, archery, poetry, flower arranging, crafts, and drama flourish today as highly developed Zen arts. Through the Japanese, Zen has become intimately intertwined with lifestyle and practice. Today the Japanese style of Zen is felt profoundly around the world.

•

Shinto: An Ancient Japanese Religion

The philosophies of ancient Japan offered fertile ground for the seeds of Chinese Zen to flower. The mysterious, misty island of early Japan was filled with forces and spirits. The original religion of Japan was Shinto, "the way of the gods." In ancient Shinto, nature had a god for everything. All aspects of nature had a corresponding spiritual form, with a god or demon that required appropriate ritual observances. Mountains, rivers, forests, waterfalls—all had their spirits. The sun goddess was the supreme ruler. According to legend, the first emperor of Japan, Jimmutenno (660 B.C.), was believed to be descended directly from this goddess, thus justifying the ancient tradition of worshipping the emperor. This spirituality, with its rituals, beliefs, and practices, is still fundamental to and intimately central within modern Japanese culture, though expressed in modern ways. The outer, superficial manifestation is a profound reverence for nature. Shinto's sprirituality directly influenced the people's

Zen has become intimately intertwined with lifestyle and practice.

receptiveness to Zen Buddhism, giving it a basis within the tapestry of culture, anchored in the family cult.

The Japanese family cult revolves around many axes, but one important feature remains constant: the family unit is primary and has authority over the life of the individual members. The family cult is ancient, linked to the early beginnings of Japan.

The ancestral cult permitted no individual freedom. No one could live according to his or her pleasure; everyone had to live according to family rules. The individual did not even have a legal existence; the family was the unit of society. [1]

The family was a patriarchy, with the father in charge as trustee for the entire family clan, which was in turn subsumed into the wider culture. The patriarch had to be intimately involved in the household, watching over all its members. After his death, his spirit continued as part of their lives, imaginatively consulted concerning decisions and judging the family's actions. He was revered to such an extent that the family made symbolic sacrifices to please him. The family cult was a subset of the communal cult.

The communal cult was bound to a pantheon of spirits who expected certain customs and behavior to be upheld. The individual was always submissive to the communal will, which could act as one person with ten thousand hands!

The early Japanese people believed that ancestral spirits could become angry and malevolent if disrespected or dishonored. Their religion had the potential to lead to tyranny and fear.

Shinto is not a formal religious doctrine but rather a collection of rituals, deities, and traditions associated with folk customs. Japanese people have retained these customs from early times. Shinto was modified in the nineteenth century, supported by restoration efforts as a means of returning Japan to its indigenous beliefs. Shinto was basic to the soul of Japan; therefore, the foreign philosophies imported from China and India (such as Taoism and Buddhism) needed to be integrated with Shinto to be accepted.

•

Introduction of Buddhism

Japan received Buddhism from Korea in A.D. 552 when the king of Paekji, one of the three kingdoms of early Korea, presented the Japanese emperor Kinmei with a gold and bronze image of Shakyamuni Buddha along with an inscription concerning its great merit and value. Japanese Prince Regent Shotoku Taishi (A.D. 572–621) became a devotee of Buddhist culture. He used it as part of his program to improve Japan, as a basis for morality, and to guide the conduct of his people.

Japan received Buddhism from Korea in A.D. 552.

The Hinayana or Theravada forms of Buddhism were never particularly attractive to the Japanese. Japan is a nation that absorbs and borrows from others, but always gives to what it assimilates a unique Japanese character as it does so. Mahayana permits this. Hinayana, with its strict adherence to the teachings of Shakyamuni Buddha, does not. Mahayana, true to its intent, openly embraces other cultures and includes them in its evolution. Japanese Buddhism recast the Shinto deities into their own pantheon and thus borrowed the power and influence without the tyranny.

The first Japanese to study Mahayana Buddhism pursued the Tendai and Shingon sects, both founded in the eighth century A.D. Tendai Buddhism was particularly successful in Japan.

Tendai, based on T'ien-t'ai from China (see p. 29), encouraged both meditation and study, mind and body, along with rituals. Many of the early Japanese Zen monks were first involved with Tendai. Eisai, who brought Zen to Japan, was a Tendai monk. Dogen, one of the most famous Japanese Zen monks, was ordained a Tendai before he learned about Zen. The interaction between the two sects continued through the centuries.

Tendai encouraged both meditation and study.

Shingon Buddhism is a Japanese form of Buddhism that was brought from China to Japan. Kukai, known as Kobo Daishi, is credited as the founder of the Japanese sect. In China, Shingon was called Chen-yen, the True Word, or Mantra, School beginning about A.D. 300. Chen-yen derived from a mystical Indian religion that views the universe as the spiritual body of the Buddha.

Shingon is a unique system of Buddhism, unlike any other in several ways, though it incorporates doctrines from Tendai and Kegon. Dharmakaya, or "body of Buddha," is basic to Shingon. Shingon holds that Buddha is enlightened, always has been, and always will be, now and forever. Logically, therefore, people can be enlightened now, in this body, in this life, and without needing millions of years in successive reincarnations, as in other systems. Also, since the universe is Buddha, everything in it is Buddha and can be a vehicle for enlightenment. Symbolic gestures, words, and actions are all the expression of Buddha and a means of enlightenment. According to Shingon doctrine, enlightenment can be expressed in words, since words are part of the Buddha's manifestation. Our everyday sensual reality of sound, smell, and taste is real in the world of Shingon, unlike in other forms of Buddhism, where nothing is real.

Shingon uses symbolic rituals, visualizations, and mantras as techniques to harmonize the practitioner's individual mind with the mind of the Buddha. Practitioners evoke the inherent state of enlightenment to mystically become one with the Buddha. The rituals are rich and elaborate and include methods of meditation, mystical verse, and recitals.

•

Early Attempts to Introduce Zen to Japan

Both Tendai and Shingon Buddhism included Zen meditation in their rituals. This set the stage for the acceptance of Zen as a separate sect that took place later. Zen Buddhism in Japan cannot be separated from the context of Japan's background in Buddhism, though Zen was to lead the country into a new direction. The transition to Zen included Tendai and Shingon rituals side by side with Zen traditions in literature, philosophy, and practice. Tendai monks taught meditation as part of their practice but believed that no one system was paramount.

Up to the Kamakura period (A.D. 1185–1333), Zen was not successfully propagated in Japan even though several Chinese monks came. Tao-hsuan Lu-shih (702–60) came from China to teach the Northern School of Ch'an that he had learned from P'u-chi (651–739), but he did not found a school of Zen in Japan, nor did he build a temple. Saichō (767–822), a well-known Japanese Buddhist monk, learned Zen meditation from a disciple of a disciple of Tao-hsuan Lu-shih, a monk who had a Tendai and Kegon Buddhist background. Saichō subsequently went to China for a year in 804 but kept his main involvement with Tendai (although he did teach meditation after his return).

Dosho (628–70), another monk who helped establish Buddhism in Japan, learned of Zen meditation from one of his Chinese teachers, Hui-man (a disciple of the Second Patriarch, Hui-k'o), when he was studying in China in 653. When he returned to Japan, he opened the first meditation hall. A man of action, Dosho was involved in charitable deeds and public works. He did not build a temple or found a line of succession.

Zen was introduced again one century later when I-k'ung (Giku in Japanese), from the line of Ma-tsu, was invited by the Empress Tachibana Kachiko, the wife of the Emperor Saga Tennō, to the Japanese court to teach. She built him a temple where he could hold instruction, but he ultimately felt discouraged with the project. On a wall at Rashoman he wrote an inscription bemoaning that Zen would never be propagated to the East. Then he left forever! Little did he imagine what the future would actually be.

•

Zen Takes Root in Japan

Myoan Eisai (1141–1215) was the founder of Zen in Japan. He was ordained as a Tendai priest and later went to China, searching for the true dharma. He hoped to reform Buddhism in Japan, where it had lost its fervor and become corrupt, partly due to priestly involvements in economics and politics. Eisai returned to China a second time (1187), intending to trace Buddhism to its original roots in India, but was denied visa privileges by Chinese authorities. He remained in China and searched for a suitable monastery in China, went to Mount Tien T'ai, and then after following his teacher Hsu-an Huai-Ch'ang (eighth generation of the Rinzai Huang-lung line) to Mount T'ien-t'ung, achieved enlightenment. Eisai was given the insignia of succession as the dharma heir, along with a certificate of enlightenment, making him the official Japanese emissary of the true dharma of the Buddha.

Upon returning to Kyoto, Eisai founded the Kennin-ji Monastery in 1202 under the patronage of the royal family, the Hojo regime. This was the first Zen temple in Japan that succeeded. There, he taught a combination of Tendai and Zen Buddhism. He was frequently in contention with Tendai Buddhists, who claimed that he had forsaken his Tendai teacher and traditions. Eisai responded ardently that he remained absolutely loyal, since Tendai, at its heart, did believe that meditation was the true path to satori. Eisai claimed that the Buddhist establishment had strayed from this truth. Furthermore, Zen possessed a special link to the "true dharma," and Eisai devoted his life to bringing this gift to Japan. His Zen teaching was mixed with Tendai training, traditions, and theory. He did not separate Zen from Tendai. Eisai continued to be at one with both until his death.

After Eisai died, one of his gifted disciples, Myozen, decided to follow in the footsteps of his teacher by making a pilgrimage to China. Most of the monks were skeptical about such a long trip. Only his student Dogen endorsed and encouraged the plan. Myozen brought his own students, including the young monk Dogen, little knowing that Dogen would later have a profound and lasting influence on Zen.

Myozen went to Mount T'ien-t'ung and stayed at the Ching-te Monastery, where his master Eisai had studied. There, Myozen studied Zen with Ju-ching and Wu-chi. He unexpectedly became very ill and passed away at this temple in China after three years, never returning to Japan. The work of his temple was carried on by Eisai's two disciples who had remained in Japan, Gyoyu and Eicho. Their backgrounds were in Shingon and Tendai Buddhism, respectively, and they faithfully carried out their duties as monks, combining Rinzai Zen with Buddhism in their teaching. Gyoyu became the abbot of Eisai's first temple, the Jufuku-ji.

Chinese Rinzai monks came to Japan to teach, and Japanese monks went to China to study and gain enlightenment so that they could return to teach in Japan. Oral transmission of teachings through face-to-face communication was most common.

In 1254, Kakushin (1207–98), one of Gyoyu's students, went to China and became a student of the Rinzai monk

Wu-men Hui-k'ai (Mumon). Kakushin returned with the famous collection of his Chinese master's koans, the *Mumonkan*. Even though Wu-men's sect of Zen is no longer in existence, his collection of koans has lived on and continues to be fundamental to formal Rinzai Zen curriculum. Many of the koans we are familiar with today come from the *Mumonkan*.

One of the pivotal monks of the thirteenth century was Enni Ben'en (1201–80). He met with unusual success when he went to China, having been accepted by a prominent Chinese Zen master, Wu-chun Shih-fan, from one of the Five Mountain Schools of Sung China. Back in Japan, Enni's fame attracted the attention of a benefactor who had a grand temple erected, called Tofuku-ji. Later this temple became one of the Five Mountain Temples of Zen in Kyoto.

Enni thought that Zen was the foundation for all Buddhism.

Enni believed that Zen was the foundation for all Buddhism including Tendai and Shingon. He explained why:

> Zen is the Buddha mind. The precepts (morality) are its external form; the teachings are its explanation in words; the invocation of the name is an expedient means. Because these three proceed from the Buddha mind, the school represents the foundation. [2]

Enni's Zen derived from the teachings of the Sixth Patriarch, Hui-neng. The Buddha-mind is without form and attachments and should not engage in any thinking, even moral judgment. He often said, "Do not think good, do not think evil." He firmly believed that learning from sutras and sastras is superficial compared with the deeper wisdom gained through the empty Buddha-mind.

Enni reached many people with his faith in pure Zen. His long life, devoted to spreading the message that Zen itself should be the foundation, helped to firmly plant Zen on Japanese soil.

Nampo believed Zen wisdom transcends the cultural context.

Nampo Shōmyō (1235–1308) was said to be Enni Ben'en's nephew. He traveled to China and experienced enlightenment at the thriving center of Chinese Zen on Mount Ching. Back in Japan, Nampo attracted many followers. He encouraged a patriotic sentiment for national responsibility and expressed it in phrases like "the Great Nation of Nippon." Even though Zen originated in China, he believed Zen wisdom transcends the cultural context. He said that the teachings of the patriarchs are timeless. Japanese should live in the here and now; Zen was brought to Japan and existed in the present moment. It was now Japanese, not a foreign Chinese philosophy. This same wisdom can be applied today in America. It comes from other roots, but Zen is here now. The line of succession formed by Nampo's disciples became two of the lines that are still influential today, Daitoku-ji and Myōshin-ji.

As Zen gradually separated from Buddhism, it was warmly received by the samurai class. People commonly said that Tendai Buddhism was for the imperial court, Shingon Buddhism for the nobility, Zen for the warriors, and Pure Land for the masses. The intertwining of Zen with martial arts has continued to the present day.

Numerous lines of Rinzai were propagated from more than twenty Chinese masters who journeyed to Japan, as well as from Japanese monks who returned from China. During the periods of Buddhist persecution in China, many talented Rinzai Zen masters went to Japan to seek new horizons and to flee the tyranny of the Mongols. This influx furthered the development of Rinzai Zen in Japan.

Corresponding to this immigration was a need in Japan to reform and revitalize the country and restore enthusiasm to the people, who had been let down by Buddhism's corruption and loss of fervor over time.

The Rinzai set out to educate the Japanese people about Zen. They did so with great discipline and careful structure, based on the Chinese model. Rinzai was taught in Japan based upon the Zen schooling methods used in China, with a hierarchy that included a major and minor authority. The administrative structure in China during the Sung dynasty was named Five Mountains, Ten Temples. The Five Mountains had authority over the cities, and the Ten Temples were a bureaucracy set up to oversee the dissemination of Zen teachings in the rural locations. Each setting had different needs and thus its own appropriate system. This system would soon be installed in Japan.

Though China evolved toward unification of all Zen sects (and eventually all Buddhism, during the later Sung and Ming dynasty periods), Japan did not embrace this movement. Japanese Zen, sprung largely from the early Sung masters, had taken root, and was becoming truly

Japanese, as is the Japanese way. The Sung and earlier T'ang Zen philosophies became part of the fabric of Japan, with a Japanese character, and were not to be altered in the syncretistic direction of the Ming period.

Japanese Zen evolved from a minor, secondary sect into an accepted, self-sufficient school. By the thirteenth century, Rinzai Zen had established complete independence and was on a par with other schools of Japanese Buddhism.

Dogen: Just Sit and Meditate

Dogen (1200–53) was the founder of Soto Zen in Japan. His single-minded zeal and absolute adherence to a strict life of only Zen inspired awe in those around him. He took Zen to its absolute extreme. He urged all to follow the Buddha Way and become monks. In taking a strong position and living it unwaveringly, Dogen had a profound influence on Zen for all time.

Dogen: the founder of Soto Zen

Dogen was born into an aristocratic Kyoto family, but his family life was not destined to be happy. Both his parents died when he was very young. The loss affected him deeply, and he vowed to become a monk to comprehend the meaning and purpose of life. At the age of thirteen he was formally initiated as a monk at a Tendai temple. Buddhism became his family and his life, but young Dogen felt uncertain why, if everyone has Buddha-nature, they must train to attain it. When the abbot could not answer him satisfactorily, Dogen continued to search. Eventually someone suggested he go to Eisai. He came to Eisai's temple and asked him his question. Eisai answered that animals are aware of their Buddha-nature, but only unenlightened ones worry about whether they have Buddha-nature. Once this is understood, there is no need to even think about it. Dogen recognized Eisai's wisdom and decided to stay at the Rinzai temple. Unfortunately, Eisai died the next year, so Dogen became the student of Eisai's disciple, Myozen. Dogen grew to be a dominating figure, with an authoritative and powerful personality.

When Myozen decided to make a pilgrimage to China, Dogen accompanied him and remained there after his teacher died. He went first to the renowned master Wu Chi at Mount T'ien-t'ung, but, after some time there, grew discouraged, as he was given a low status and did not achieve enlightenment. He traveled about China and went to various monks and temples to experience and study. As he was about to leave, he was told of the new abbot at Mount T'ien-t'ung, Ju-ching (1163–1228), the monk who had taught Myozen, an outspoken opponent of Rinzai and koan-introspectioninst schools. Training at Ju-ching's temple was severe. Dogen sat in *zazen* until his whole body ached, but as he said, "I liked zazen so much the better!" [3] One morning when Dogen was beginning his formal zazen session for the day, Ju-ching chided another monk for dozing. He said that the practice of zazen is the dropping-away of mind and body, so what could be accomplished by dozing? Hearing these words, Dogen was enlightened. He was given a certificate of transmission, the robe of his teacher's teacher, some texts by a Ts'ao-tung master, and a picture of Ju-ching.

Ju-ching also gave Dogen four recommendations: avoid

kings or their ministers, spread Buddhism forever, live in the country, and avoid the cities and other populated areas.

Dogen returned to Japan in 1227 with Ju-ching's blessings, but was not to follow his teacher's instructions. He settled at Kennin-ji for three years and attempted to influence Japanese national policy. He proclaimed optimistically to the government that Zen would lead to the evolution of Japanese society because of its positive emphasis on equality and unity among all people. Unsuccessful in his political efforts, Dogen eventually gave up this quest and returned to his regular duties.

Dogen grew dissatisfied with the lifestyle of the Rinzai monks at Kennin-ji. He considered the monk's life to be too luxurious (for example, five chests of clothing and possessions for the monks, as well as improper permissiveness toward their manners). He moved out after writing a short treatise on Zen practice and went to another temple, where he had a meditation hall built. His fame grew.

Dogen lived a virtuous life, with a strict code of conduct based on his understanding of Zen: Practice and enlightenment are one. He carefully spelled out in detail how to behave as a monk: give up all worldly attachment and sit in zazen. [4]

Dogen believed that to become a monk was the highest and most important calling in life. He roundly praised the monkish vow of extreme poverty as essential for all monks, to the point of insisting that to achieve enlightenment, one must wear a *kasaya,* or monk's robe. Dogen considered the robe to be a powerful symbol in itself. He claimed that even the famous emperors should wear one. It was best if the

Dogen believed that to become a monk was the highest and most important calling in life.

kasaya was pieced together from castaway rags—the dirtier and more disgusting, the better—as a corrective to the common tendency of people to be caught up in luxury and finery. He felt that nonattachment to material things was fundamental in Buddhism.

Dogen believed that practice cannot be separated from enlightenment. They are one. He used words, and even the structure of language itself, to give profound experiences. Language was zazen to Dogen. Koan was zazen. All methods could lead to the realization of enlightenment. He thought that neither ritualistic recitation of sutras nor earnest contemplation of koans for their true essence would lead to enlightenment, because they are already identical to it. Duality is an illusion. Dogen believed that the use of koans was unnecessary, but he would allow his students to use them, if they wished, as a means of concentrating their attention. The merit of koans is that they are the expression of enlightenment.

Until the moment of his death at age fifty-three, Dogen zealously proclaimed that it is important to follow the path of enlightenment at all times, never wavering from it for anything. His last writing courageously proclaimed an injunction to earnestly practice zazen and never waver. He hoped to be reborn in circumstances that would allow him to return immediately to Zen meditation. His commitment transcended life itself.

Dogen fully embraced Zen Buddhism, living in an exemplary manner. He urged Zen students to devote themselves wholeheartedly—mind, body, and spirit—to Zen. He urged followers of the Way to discard their relationships and all worldly goods and join a temple. Dogen said:

> Buddhism differs completely from the usual ways of the world . . . for monks, then, the ways of the world should be shunned. [5]

Dogen believed strongly in absolute dedication to Buddhism. He considered any ties, whether to family or even to concern for life itself, secondary and potential hindrances. Emotional attachment should be of little concern to the monk. Be indifferent about everything except being a humble monk, practicing Zen Buddhism. Complete poverty is the Buddha Way, Dogen assured his followers.

Dogen's message was reassuring to the struggling masses, among whom starvation and poverty were common. They could be transformed, happy, and at peace even though they were poor. Dogen proclaimed, like Hui-neng, that the Way is open to anyone, whether bright or stupid, good or bad. Even some of the disciples of the Buddha had been evil at times. This means that it is possible for anyone and everyone to be redeemed.

Dogen proclaimed that the Way is open to anyone.

Dogen's way was simple and consistent. He urged his students to serve the cause of Buddhism above all else: personal gain is an obstruction. Enter a monastery, give up the search for fame and profit—the seeker will surely find the Way. This life *now* is the life you have been given and thus the path to enlightenment. There is no other. Empty the mind of personal views of any kind. Arguments of doctrine, conduct, position, or authority are all irrelevant and delusional. Follow unwaveringly the Buddha Way, and all conflict dissolves; you can be filled with the waters of enlightenment.

Dogen was a strict and spartan disciplinarian. He was stern and demanding concerning the necessity to strive unceasingly in the pursuit of Buddhist goals. The intense, disciplined zeal that Dogen inspired is highly respected and fundamental in Zen as it is practiced today, though considerable moderation was needed to make it applicable to life in modern culture as it evolved. Today, from Dogen's simple beginnings, without even a temple or center, Soto Zen has become a worldwide movement.

The cornerstone of Dogen's approach is to practice zazen.

The cornerstone of Dogen's approach is to practice zazen, sitting in meditation. He emphasized this above all else. He believed that not to cling to anything, to be nonattached, is a primary guiding principle. He advised his followers not to follow teachings that are incorrect:

> From this we can see the importance of discerning the truth and of not always accepting the words of ancient Masters. Although it is not good to take a suspicious attitude, it is also a mistake to cling to something that does not deserve faith and not to question meaning that should be explored. [6]

Dogen's Zen broke away from reliance on learning from sutras or other literature as the central determiner of enlightenment. In life, there is no real existence of sutras and thus no nonexistence to worry about either, so students of Zen need not fear the sutras and avoid them due to concern that they may be misleading.

Dogen's talks in his *Shobogenzo* repeatedly exhorted listeners to find the basis for ethics and values through sitting in Zen meditation rather than through studying foreign philosophies such as Confucianism and Taoism. [7] Dogen ultimately did not deny the importance of conduct and action as fundamental, but he denied its Confucian basis. In fact, he was adamantly opposed to both Confucianism and Taoism:

> Among present-day Chinese monks, there is not even one who is aware that the teachings of Confucius and Lao-tsu are inferior to those of the Buddha . . . . Those who slander the Buddha by thinking that his teachings are the same as those of Confucius and Lao-tsu will not have to wait until their next life to reap the karmic retribution of their crime! Should we trainees fail to discard this false view quickly, we too will end by falling into hell. [8]

Dogen believed that the traditional virtues of Confucianism, such as filial piety, are not correct for Zen monks. Sitting in meditation should take precedence over any loyalties the monk may have. Dogen insisted that it is not necessary for Zen monks to adapt foreign philosophies for use in guiding conduct. The guide for conduct can be found in the practice of zazen itself.

The substitute Dogen offered for Confucianism's social ethic was to receive and follow the precepts along with Buddhism's codes of conduct. The precepts include specific rules to follow for conduct and morality. Receiving the precepts was the first step to entering the Way, according to Dogen.

This is done in a ceremony between the initiate and the master. The initiate burns incense, prostrates himself in front of the master, and asks permission to receive the precepts. Once permission is granted, the ceremony begins.

First, the student recites the traditional vows of Buddhism: I take refuge in the Buddha, I take refuge in the Dharma, I take refuge in the Sangha. These vows are repeated three times. Next, the initiate recites three precepts regarding moral behavior and swears to follow them: do not do evil, do good, and help others. Then the initiate commits himself to the ten prohibitions: He must not kill, steal, engage in sex, lie, drink intoxicating beverages, or speak of the faults of bodhisattvas. He should never be too proud to praise others, should never covet property, should never give way to anger or criticize the Three Treasures (the Buddha, the Dharma, the Sangha). The ceremony ends with the initiate swearing that he will uphold all these precepts.

Dogen was adamant that it is not correct for a monk to seek enlightenment without receiving the precepts. As he said, "How can you expect to become a Buddha if you do not guard against faults and prevent yourself from doing wrong?" [9] Dogen believed that enlightenment without commitment to the precepts is not true enlightenment. A good monk is a moral monk.

Dogen passed his succession to Koun Ejo (1198–1280), a sincere seeker of the Way. Ejo had been ordained in Tendai Buddhism, which permitted Zen meditation to have a place. Fascinated by the deeper consciousness he found through meditation, Ejo joined a small sect of Zen known as Daruma and experienced enlightenment. The Daruma School was attacked by other sects during competitive and turbulent times and was finally forced to disperse after the temple was burned down by Tendai monks. Ejo sought out Dogen and had long talks with him. Recognizing Dogen's wisdom, Ejo asked the master to accept him as his disciple, but Dogen said the time was not yet right. Ejo returned to his ailing Daruma teacher, Kakuan, and cared for him until the teacher's death.

After years of patient waiting, Ejo was accepted by Dogen and became a devoted disciple. The master-disciple relationship was very close. Ejo helped Dogen compile his *Shobogenzo* by recording and editing his master's lectures.

Following Dogen's death, Ejo carried on his master's pure teachings as best he could, although he lacked the strong personality of Dogen. Problems developed as a result of the third generation heir, Tettsu Gikai (1219–1309), who had been designated by Dogen himself. Ejo dutifully passed the succession to Gikai, despite his misgivings. When Gikai undertook ambitious temple-building projects to attract new adherents, Dogen's other disciples became angry, disappointed, and alienated by this about-face in policy; they believed Gikai's choices were contrary to the spartan spirit of Dogen. Divisions developed, resulting in at least five lines of Soto Zen, some of which continue to this day.

Dogen's influence waxed and waned after his death but was revived several generations later. Many lines of Soto Zen evolved. Modern Japanese Soto eventually unified the lines, through Dogen's clear statements and explicit teachings. His influence has been profound and lasting on Zen for all time.

In the early 1900s, a Dogen revival began that has engaged some of the best minds of modern philosophy. (This revival is described in greater depth in Chapter Five, "Transitions.")

The two main, dominant sects of Zen became Rinzai and Soto. As in China, Japanese Rinzai emphasized the koan as a means of bringing the mind to enlightenment through successive states and insights. Soto stressed the experience of zazen, of meditation itself, as central and necessary to continuously practice. Satori, the experience of enlightenment, was emphasized in Rinzai but not in Soto. Both sects used koans and concentration of the mind in meditation, but each emphasized their function differently. They disagreed in doctrine and contended with each other, sometimes bitterly.

•

The Middle Period (1200–1600)

Gozan: City Zen

During the thirteenth century, the Rinzai school became institutionalized by the state into the three-tiered system composed of "Five Mountains" (*gozan*), "Ten Temples" (*jissetsu*), and many larger temples (*shozan*), with headquarters in Kyoto and Kamakura. A national teacher, Muso (1275–1351), was appointed and recognized by seven emperors; even though Japanese politics was in flux, all the leaders recognized Muso. He was central in helping to spread Zen despite the many civil wars of the times.

During the Middle Period, the shogun embraced Zen

Buddhism, and emperors frequently supported a temple with a Zen monk set up as the abbot. From Kyoto and Kamakura, Rinzai Zen branched out into rural community settings as well. The number of enthusiastic adherents steadily grew. Numerous teachers and anonymous monks guided the development of Zen—their works helped spread the teachings. During this period of growth, emperors, feudal lords, and shoguns built many temples in Kamakura, Kyoto, and provinces throughout the country. Zen philosophy continued to be used in an attempt to unify the country, which was torn apart by internal battles for power. Zen acted as a stabilizing influence and a source of inspiration.

Zen competed with the established Buddhist temples for the favor of royalty. The Zen monks gained support and patronage from artists, warriors, merchants, and intellectuals. In turn, the Zen monks did their part for the country, offering education, collecting funds for their patrons' military, and giving shelter and assistance to artists.

National Teacher Muso

Muso Soseki began his Buddhist training in Shingon Buddhism but made a radical conversion to Zen after the painful death of his Shingon teacher. He realized then that the problems of life and death could not be solved by education alone. After one hundred days in silent meditation, he decided to study Zen. He went to many masters to study, eventually settling in with the famous Chinese master I-shan. But even though the content of the teachings was Zen, Muso was not satisfied that he was on the right path. He left and wandered from monastery to monastery, seeking out many different instructors. His enlightenment did not come within a temple. Rather, his awakening happened while he was in a garden. Thinking he would lean against a wall, Muso lost his balance and fell over. With this, the "wall of darkness" disappeared. Muso found what he was looking for. He wrote the following poem about it.

> For many years I dug the earth and searched for the blue
> heaven,
> And how often, how often did my heart grow heavier and
> heavier.
> One night, in the dark, I took stone and brick,
> And mindlessly struck the bones of the empty heavens. [10]

Muso's enlightenment did not come in a temple, but in a garden.

Muso returned to a former teacher, Koho Kennichi, for confirmation. Kennichi, impressed with his enlightenment, gave Muso the Seal of Dharma. Following his enlightenment, Muso traveled to many small hermitages. He valued meditation in solitude. Throughout his busy and involved life he periodically departed to travel and be alone.

Muso's transient lifestyle of solitude was altered forever when he was called by Emperor Go-Daigo to become the abbot of the most prominent Zen monastery, Nanzen-ji in Kyoto. But Emperor Go-Daigo's rule was short (1334–36), and when Ashikaga Takauji was appointed shogun in 1338, a new phase of Japanese history, the Ashikaga period, began (1338–1573).

Muso played an important part in the early Ashikaga

period, bringing official imperial recognition to Zen and helping to codify the monastic traditions. He wrote a collection of guidelines for monasteries and monks called *Rinsen Kakun* and *San'e-in yuikai* (1339) and *Saihō yuikai* (1345). He prescribed four hours of zazen meditation every day. Sutras and rituals were inferior to zazen practice. He believed in the strict discipline of the early patriarchs.

Muso was not only an organizer, he was also a devoted Zen teacher. He expressed his views clearly in writings and verse. He believed in the use of koans but felt that they were only a means to an end and might not be necessary for everyone. Zen should embrace all of life, he taught; thus, all activities of life can serve as a means to practice. Meditation should include, but not be limited to, seated zazen. This theme continues in modern Zen today. Over the years Muso served at a number of monasteries and oversaw the building of new temples. He transformed corrupt, unruly monasteries into thriving, serious centers for Zen practice. His later development as a Zen teacher reflects his Shingon background. Since everything is Buddha, everything and anything can be a vehicle of enlightenment.

This dynamic individual left an indelible mark on Japanese Zen. He remains an example of enlightened wisdom, always intellectually independent despite the many pressures he must have felt in his high position. His final verse left to his disciples was the following:

With one stroke I erase my delay in the transient world.
What does this mean? Yasa! [11]

Despite Zen's insistence on being beyond words and letters, many fine literary works were created during this middle period. Poetry, art, and literature all developed, embryonic phases of the many Zen arts that have been one of Japan's finest contributions to the Zen spirit.

Although the Gozan period eventually went into decline because of changes in the political climate, civil wars, and unrest, Zen moved forward to evolve further through traditions outside the Five Mountains system.

Rinka: Rural Zen

Rinzai

While the Five Mountains system spread throughout the cities during the Gozan period, there were other large monasteries located in the rural areas. These numerous temples all around the countryside became centers for the development and flowering of Zen arts as well as some of the most distinguished lines of Japanese Zen.

The lines of succession evolved in the country under the patronage of the rulers as they came to utilize the monasteries and monks for their needs. The Japanese were ingenious in finding methods to make practical use of Zen. Following the Zen "Way" allowed artists, swordsmen, poets, and painters to develop specialized paths to follow, with definite techniques, including the Way of Archery, the Way of Flowers, and the most well-known, the Way of the Martial Arts. Zen was used to serve society, and such functions as educating the people, raising money for the samurai, and working out negotiations with the Chinese, were conducted by the monks.

Shuho Myocho (1282–1338), the founder of Daitoku-ji (Great Virtue), one of the influential Rinzai lines, was a student of Nampo of the Kamakura era (1185–1333). After his enlightenment, Shuho spent time in Kyoto devoting himself to helping others. In a well-known legend, the emperor Hanazono heard of an unusual beggar in Kyoto and decided to personally find out the truth about him. He brought with him a basket of melons that Shuho happened to like. The emperor addressed the group that was gathered around the beggar and said, "I will give a melon to anyone who can step up without using his feet." Shuho immediately stood up and said, "Then give me a melon without using your hands!" The emperor was so impressed with Shuho's quick response that he brought him to the palace, and they began a long and warm relationship. In one conversation the emperor said to Shuho, "Is it not amazing that the Buddha-dharma is facing the royal dharma on the same level?" Shuho replied, "Is it not amazing that the royal dharma is facing the Buddha-dharma on the same level?" The emperor, who was an insightful ruler, appreciated the wisdom of this exchange.

In 1327, the emperor gave Shuho a temple with land and made him national master. Several years later the emperor elevated Shuho's Daitoku-ji to the rank of first temple alongside the Gozan system. The Daitoku-ji Zen School believed that it was better to be someone who spends the day in the field, eating damp vegetables boiled in a rickety kettle, than to live in luxury in an elaborate monastery, surrounded by portraits of Buddha encased in gold. The value of simplicity, which matured within the Daitoku-ji temples, has become the cornerstone of Zen arts. These temples were also centers for tea ceremonies, had beautiful gardens, and were sanctuaries for numerous Zen painters. Shuho himself was one of Japan's foremost calligraphers.

Shuho recommended that one of his students, Kanzan Egen (1277–1360), be given a new monastery. Emperor Hanazono presented Kanzan with a temple on his estate so that the emperor could learn Zen. This temple, Myoshin-ji, was unpretentious, small, with a leaky roof. Only those with a true commitment to Zen could persevere despite the hardships. Many prominent Zen masters studied there, including Hakuin Ekaku (1689–1769), who was to revolutionize Zen.

Soto

Although the temple system was arranged in order, the system of teaching was not. Deeply felt differences in doctrines were not easily resolved. Feuds between Ch'an sects in China were brought over to Japan along with Zen, especially the dispute between the Soto and Rinzai sects of Zen. Even though enlightenment was a shared value, Soto was more similar to the Northern system, and Rinzai more closely resembled the Southern style. Each had different interpretations and emphases.

The Rinzai monks emphasized action—dynamic, energetic, simple—yet searched constantly to deepen and improve enlightenment. Koans were important and were individualized in the style of the early Chinese masters. By contrast, Soto emphasized focused attention, such as sitting in Zen meditation, referred to as *shikantaza,* together with pious morality. Soto used every experience, every activity, to awaken the mind to enlightenment. The Soto monks did not use koans as an object of study outside the meditative state. Soto doctrine held that koans, like anything, could be a means of focusing the mind in meditation, but were not special. Attention to the details of everyday life can bring and maintain enlightenment in Soto practice.

Soto Zen also expanded during the middle period. There were at least three major lines of Soto. Like the Rinzai monks, the Soto monks manifested the bodhisattva ideal of a genuine love for humanity by performing community service. Gasan Jōseki, in direct line from Dogen, engendered a strong social conscience in a large number of devoted monks. They ventured out among the impoverished rural population to help the people with their education and welfare.

Gasan's style of Zen returned to the Five Ranks from the Soto House of Sung China but gave them a practical Japanese character. The changes Gasan made helped students understand the meaning that the Buddha-dharma gave to their everyday world.

As Soto developed into a popular religion, it retained Dogen's emphasis on zazen meditation. Regular practice of meditation made sense to the common people. Much of the population became involved with special clubs, like community centers, that were formed to bring meditation directly to the people. The monks also did their part to help in tangible ways. They went out in the fields with the farmers, helped build bridges, irrigate rice fields, and drain swamps.

Many lines of Zen, both Rinzai and Soto, flourished under numerous dynamic masters. Through the middle period many talented people were drawn to the sanctuary of Zen, where they could devote themselves with absolute dedication to their art or to the service of others. Zen journeyed from the temples into the community to give, and the community journeyed to the temples to receive.

•

Full Flowering of Japanese Zen

The Tokugawa era (1603–1867) marks the beginning of the feudal period in Japan. [12] Just before this era, Lord Oda Nobunaga (1534–82) had embarked on a comprehensive campaign to eradicate Buddhism from Japan. Nobunaga felt that the Buddhist temples had accumulated too much power. Many monasteries even retained their own armies. He resolved to crush Buddhism and embarked on a purge not unlike the one in China in the ninth century. Buddhist temples were burned, thousands of monks were killed or driven out from the Tendai, Shingon, and Pure Land sects. Only Zen retained a high standing in Japanese society, as the keeper of the arts and education. This helped bring about Zen's ascendancy over the other schools of Buddhism in Japan.

Zen gained ascendancy over the other schools of Buddhism in Japan.

Rinzai Zen monks tended to be literate and cultured, familiar with the language and customs of the Chinese. They were expected to be ethical, impartial, and above petty disputes. The Zen temples were also given the role of helping educate the masses in academic subjects and Confucian studies at the monasteries. Zen practice was kept clearly separated. The monasteries often taught Zen in the morning and Confucian studies in the evening. The fact that the Zen monks were educated in the Confucian classics and guides to conduct made them valuable to the shoguns and emperors. The monks could easily communicate as diplomats with Chinese and Koreans who also used these codes of behavior. They knew how to perform the rituals used in diplomacy. Zen monks helped work out diplomatic negotiations and trade agreements with China.

The monastery schools contributed positively to the overall level of education in the country. The social engineers of Japan continued to utilize Zen as a basic part of the effort to help its people evolve and be secure.

For all of these reasons, the Tokugawa rulers widely supported Zen and encouraged their samurai to utilize the doctrines, which were helpful in overcoming the fear of death. *Hagakure,* the definitive text of the code of the samurai, refers in several places to Zen doctrines as a guide for appropriate behavior in facing death and in dealing with life. Samurai should meet life and death fearlessly. "When meeting difficult situations, one should dash forward, bravely and with joy. It is the crossing of a single barrier and is like the saying, 'the more the water, the higher the boat.'" [13] Feudalism was prolonged in Japan by the determined, ambitious shogunate until the restoration of the emperor in the nineteenth century.

Rinzai had grown complex and elaborate. Koans became philosophical exercises, and rituals were practiced that derived from Tendai and Confucian traditions. Unlike Dogen's Soto, Rinzai was more involved with Confucianism, particularly the ideals of the Neo-Confucianists. Rinzai monks found parallels with Confucianist doctrines wherever possible; there was no fundamental conflict between Zen and Confucianism. Buddha-mind and filial piety were identical in Rinzai Zen.

Takuan Soho (1573–1645) was an influential Rinzai Zen teacher who wrote about the integration of Neo-Confucian doctrine with Zen. He also wrote about the unity of Buddhism with Shinto, stating that Buddha and *kami* (divine forces in Shinto) were simply different names for the same reality. The true reality must always be the self, the mind. He drew from the poem by the Third Chinese Patriarch, Seng-ts'an—"Words Inscribed on the Believing Mind"—meaning that the enlightened mind overcomes duality; all virtues are interrelated. It is our task as human beings to practice them all harmoniously. Takuan had a profound influence on two generations of shoguns. He guided the Zen development of several famous swordsmen, such as Yagyu Munenori and Miyamoto Musashi.

The shogunate government used Zen monasteries to help raise money to support their samurai as well as to train them in mental and spiritual discipline. Many sons of noblemen became monks; some of the rulers retired to monastic life after their service to the government. The Way of the Samurai was influenced by Zen and in turn became an influence on Zen. The actions of the samurai were to be performed with loyalty and duty as well as with deep commitment, just as the monks performed their actions with deep commitment. Takuan and other Zen teachers taught the samurai to face life and death with the requisite serious and honorable attitude. They had to be willing to die in combat, if necessary, for honor, or at the demand of the shogun in whose service the samurai was retained. This practical application of Zen training was a forerunner of our modern applied approach to Zen, offering Paths for Westerners to follow. Today, Zen may be experienced through one of the many Zen arts.

Bankei (1622–93) was a Rinzai master who was also on good terms with Soto monks. He preached to an estimated fifty thousand people in his lifetime and founded or restored some fifty to sixty temples. He held large retreats attended by more than a thousand participants, including both Rinzai and Soto disciples. Bankei's classes and lectures were open to all. His writings admonished students for paying too much attention to koan study and not enough to clearing the mind through meditation.

Bankei believed that the Unborn Mind is the basis for everything, the beginning for everything. It is prior to any belief or assumption and exists without anger or passions. Bankei encouraged everyone to stay in the Unborn Mind state. Bankei did not believe in systematizing ideas and concepts. He warned that with any construct devised by humankind, a pattern always evolves. When the pattern becomes fixed, the natural flow of life is blocked. Zen ceases to be Zen.

Bankei's way of moderation included following the way of Confucian virtues, especially honoring parents, who made it possible for you to achieve enlightenment by caring for you as a child. Bankei states:

> **Bankei believed that the Unborn Mind is the basis for everything.**

> When you are in accord with the way of filial piety, your mind
> is the Buddha–mind. Don't think because we speak of a mind
> of filial piety and a Buddha-mind that they represent two dif-
> ferent minds. There is only the one single mind, and it's di-
> rectly conversant with all things." [14]

Bankei emphasized that love and honor of the parents,
along with gratitude for what they have done, is natural and
in accord with the Unborn Mind state of Zen.

Bankei's path to enlightenment was straightforward, almost easy. He told people all they had to do was simply stay in
the Buddha-mind.

> If everyone just stays in the Buddha-mind, that's all they have
> to do—that takes care of everything. Why do you want to go
> and think up other things to do? There's no need to. Just
> dwell in the Unborn. [15]

Bankei taught that there is hope for both men and
women equally. The Buddha did not discriminate; anyone
could achieve enlightenment. Everyone has a Buddha-mind.
Even a wicked person is capable of getting in touch with
Buddha-mind and changing for the better. The Buddha-
mind can transcend good and evil and has its own wisdom
that can naturally guide people away from bad conduct, toward a virtuous life. When people return to the Unborn
Mind, it permits them to respond appropriately, restore
their morality, and change their lives for the better. Bankei's
universal appeal offered salvation and hope to all. His theory

bridged the gap between sects and helped pave the way for modern Zen's doctrine of Oneness.

Hakuin: Satori Is Only the Beginning

During the Tokugawa era, a dynamic and outspoken individual was born who would change the course of Zen forever: Hakuin Ekaku (1689–1769). A Rinzai monk, he was intense, impulsive, and fiercely idealistic, with a strong, authoritarian manner. Hakuin is considered the father of modern Rinzai Zen. The scope and breadth of his achievements were and are far-reaching. After the lamp of enlightenment was lit within him, Hakuin was impelled to reform Zen and organize the koans into a system, a Path for seekers to follow to the ultimate satori (enlightenment). He urged his students to turn away from other philosophies and turn toward Zen. He believed in satori above all else but also in the deepening of satori through continued daily systematic and disciplined study of the koans in thought, word, and deed. Hakuin also emphasized that morality was essential: with no morality, practice becomes insincere and the likely result is failure in the quest for ever greater enlightenment.

Hakuin

Hakuin believed that a healthy body is important to carry practice to completion. He recommended a set of Taoist visualization exercises that he had learned from a hermit monk who helped him recover from an illness. Hakuin faithfully used these techniques throughout the rest of his eighty-two years:

> I always direct my heart so that it fills my abdomen. Helping

students or receiving visitors or entertaining guests, however it may be, preaching or teaching and all else, I have never ceased to do it. Now in my old age the virtue of the practice is clearly apparent. . . . The point is to keep the fundamental Ki within, pervading and supporting the whole body so that in the 360 joints and 84,000 pores there is not a hair's breadth without it. Know this to be the secret of preserving life. [16]

The youngest of five children, Hakuin had an excellent memory. It is said that he memorized the entire text of the Lotus Sutra when he was eight years old! He experienced a mental breakdown at age nine that probably awakened in him the search for enlightenment early in life. He wandered for years on a religious pilgrimage and learned from many teachers until he met Shoju Rojin (1642–1721), the teacher he came to revere most. At the age of thirty-one, Hakuin had sequestered himself away in a remote mountain hermitage when he was called back home to his ailing father and asked to fill a vacancy at the local village temple, Shoin-ji. This was far from a prized position, since the temple was broken down and insignificant, a subtemple of a subtemple. Hakuin took the position and, except for the years that he traveled for his religious studies, he remained there in his hometown, Hara, a small farming village. From that base, he changed Rinzai Zen forever.

Hakuin's devotion to practice was intense. For the first ten years at Shoin-ji, he refused to sleep in a bed. He spent every night sitting in meditation, wrapped in a futon that was tied tightly around him by the young boys studying at his temple. When he fell asleep, he remained upright in meditation, searching within for ever brighter enlightenment. In the morning, the boys returned to untie him.

Although Hakuin received his first satori at age twenty-four, he had numerous other satori experiences, large and small; he knew he had much more to learn. He continued searching, not yet satisfied, until he had a decisive enlightenment in 1729, when he was forty-one. He described the experience in his autobiography, *Wild Ivy:*

> A cricket made a series of churrs at the foundation stones of the temple. The instant they reached the master's ears, he was one with enlightenment. [17]

All beings are from the very beginning Buddhas. It is like water and ice: Apart from water, no ice. Outside living beings, no Buddhas.
–Hakuin, from "Song of Meditation"

All doubts and uncertainties that he had suffered up to this point disappeared. He felt absolutely free. After this profound realization he was able to reach beyond himself to help others.

He began to accept students, a few at first, but his reputation grew steadily until he was considered the foremost Zen master in the land. Hundreds converged on his tiny temple for instruction, but because the monastery was so small, the numerous seekers had to stay in houses nearby. The effect of the continual influx of ardent students was to transform the entire area into an expansive, renowned center for Zen practice. The common saying by the townspeople was that their area had two things of greatness: Mount Fuji and Zen Master Hakuin.

Students were in awe of Hakuin, who stood as a towering, menacing presence, stalking the temple like a ferocious tiger. Yet somehow he inspired them to endure his harsh, cryptic words and the stinging blows from his stick in order to follow their Zen quest. Students who first arrived in perfect health became thin and drawn after years of Zen practice. Unaware and unconcerned, they strove mightily on the Path, a living testament to their absolute devotion to Hakuin's Way.

Hakuin had a kindly, warm side to his personality that he expressed toward his family and the townspeople. Unlike the strict code of Soto that prohibited family involvements, Hakuin's Rinzai teaching encouraged the practice of filial piety. He remained devoted to his own mother after his father's death. Whenever he could spare time away from his students, he reached out to help the townspeople, educating them through writing and painting. He created a thousand or more works of painting and calligraphy for charity, often boldly innovative.

As the years passed, Hakuin became more and more active. He wrote and taught widely and continued to practice calligraphy with great zeal. His most active period was during his last twenty-five years of life. He left more than fifty written works, ranging from complex discourses in Chinese to simple songs and chants, bringing Zen to both the educated elite and the common people.

Hakuin also continued the sectarian disputes between Soto and Rinzai. He was a committed reformer who felt that the Soto sect had become corrupt. He took a strong stand in defense of Hui-neng, the Sixth Chinese Patriarch, and against the Amida Buddhist sect, a popular movement of the time.

Hakuin could be bold and blunt in his selective appraisals. His talks made it quite clear what he judged to be true Zen and what was false. He expressed his views boldly and persuasively.

Hakuin used analogy and metaphor to instruct, pointing his students energetically toward true understanding. He discouraged aspirants from taking his words literally and thereby tying their meaning down. He shocked and entertained, thus giving pause to his listeners through audacious, colorfully expressed, and sometimes highly judgmental comparisons between awakened mind and ordinary deluded perception. This was in line with the classical tradition of the Chinese masters Lin-chi and Ma-tsu. He stirred his listeners emotionally to bring about strong reactions. Through all his intensity, he had a sense of humor:

> Now let it not be said that the old dodderer of Shoin-ji has with his dying gasps chronicled a mass of drivel to bamboozle good men. For those who are already spiritual ashes, whose blow has struck through to satori, for those higher ones this was never meant; but to dullards like myself, who have been ill like me, it will undoubtedly be of help if studied. The only fear is that outsiders may clap their hands and laugh over it. When the horse is chewing up an old straw basket, one can't get a nap in peace. [18]

Hakuin did not believe that sudden enlightenment was a terminus or endpoint to strive for but was the mind's instrument to keep evolving and growing wiser. He stressed the koan as fundamental in this process. He considered koans the highest form of Zen. They were meant to be used to help monks continue developing their enlightenment. Hakuin believed that the "Great Doubt" that came about through koan practice took precedence over all else. To help students on the Path, he created the famous koan "What is the sound of one hand clapping?" One experience of enlightenment is only the beginning. The journey is endless.

He organized the koans into categories that permitted a hierarchical curriculum to be developed for teaching the Rinzai approach to Zen. Each level was to be mastered before moving on to the next. The first group, beginning with the "one hand clapping" koan, addresses the absolute nature of reality. These koans, called *dharmakaya* koans (*hosshin* koans), were concerned with the level of realizing universal unity: All is one. Here is one example of a *hosshin* koan:

> When Ummon (Yun-men [864–949]) was asked, "What is the pure Dharma Kaya?" he replied, "The flowering hedge [surrounding the privy]." [19]

Absolute Oneness is only part of the whole, since reality is differentiated into the "ten thousand things." The second level consists of *kikan* koans, which help students comprehend how unity manifests itself in the multifaceted world of many things. Students learn that they should not stop with a single enlightenment; they must delve deeper. Here is a kikan koan:

> One who has realized his original nature escapes from

birth-and-death. When the light of your eyes falls to the ground, how will you escape? [20]

The third group is called *gonsen* level koans. At this level, students explore language, studying how language can complicate understanding and lead us astray. Despite Bodhidharma's prescription for Zen, "a special transmission outside the scriptures not founded on words and letters," Zen requires students at this level to discover how to use words to free the mind. For example,

> A monk asked Master Joshū (Chao-chou 778–897): "What is Joshū?"
> "East Gate, West Gate, South Gate, North Gate," Joshū replied. [21]

The fourth level, the *nanto* koans, are more obscure and difficult to master. This story illustrates the difficulty:

> It's like a buffalo passing through a lattice window. Its head and four legs and its body have passed through, but the tail cannot pass. Why is it that the tail cannot pass through? [22]

The fifth level of koans, known as the *goi*, are a series of fifty koans drawn from the Five Houses period in China. These koans incorporate Chinese Soto master Tung-shan's (Japanese: Tosan [807–69]) Five Ranks, which Rinzai recognized. (See Chapter Four on China). These koans deal with the relationship between the absolute and the relative, which Rinzai recognized as profound, reflecting a philosophy in which the interrelationship between mind and matter is expressed. Through the Five Ranks, that interrelationship is experienced and developed, as is the way of Rinzai Zen.

Hakuin felt that the primary koan that everyone must penetrate is Mu. Zen teacher and abbot John Daido Loori has written that all seven hundred koans are simply variations on Mu. When Mu is understood, all koans are understood. [23]

With the koan system, teachers could provide structure and direction to koan study rather than continuing the vague individualizing that, over time, inevitably led to difficulties. Hakuin's disciple Gasan Jito (1727–97) and later heirs Inzan Ien (1751–1814) and Takuju Kosen (1760–1833) continued to organize, categorize, and systematize the koan learning experience. The practice of a private verbal koan instruction between master and student was instituted. Standardized answers were developed, as were appropriate capping phrases, referred to as *jakugo,* indicating formally that the student had comprehended the koan with an acceptable interpretation. The use of graded koans and answers became a central part of the curriculum of the modern Rinzai learning experience.

Hakuin believed in searching for the source of the light, not just bathing in the illumination's glow. Thus, he enjoined all to continue to meditate deeply on the koan, striving to penetrate its core. Hakuin proclaimed the timeless virtues of dharma and of Zen above all else. He was successful at this noble task. He brought his fervor and zeal to the study of Zen. Through his dynamic and dedicated life, he became a

A monk asked Joshū, a Chinese Zen master: Has a dog Buddha-nature or not? Joshū answered: mu.

symbol for the reform of Zen, risking all to take a stand for what he believed in.

> It isn't a question of choosing a koan, scrutinizing it once, and penetrating it. If you work on it relentlessly, with unflagging devotion, you will penetrate it whether you want to or not . . . and there is nothing that could bring you such intense joy and satisfaction. [24]

Hakuin's spirit and character permeate the Zen of today. We all continue to hear the sound of one hand clapping: Hakuin's hand.

•

Meiji Period (1868–1912)

Japan underwent a major transition during the Meiji period. With the removal of the Tokugawa shogunate, the emperor system was restored. Japan opened itself to the outside world, becoming part of the international community.

Certain changes in the religious policies affected Buddhism very deeply. Corruption and moral laxity had crept into the Buddhist temples, angering Japanese society. By the end of the Tokugawa period, riots broke out, temples were burned, and people demanded reform. The Meiji government responded by trying to restore the indigenous Shinto religion. They created a national institution that at first did not include any Buddhist participation at all. Eventually it was modified to become the Ministry of Religion and Education. Shinto, Confucianism, and Buddhism were represented, although Buddhists had a lesser role.

The government introduced other innovations, hoping to help Buddhism reform. Marriage for all Buddhist monks was one of the changes. Buddhism did reform, and Zen meditation became more popular than ever.

One of the Meiji government's goals was to create a national education system. They called upon the Soto Zen monks to help. In 1870 all existing schools in Japan, from elementary through professional schools, were run by Soto Zen monks. They taught Zen Buddhist doctrine along with Chinese studies, English, and mathematics. However, the monastery schools could not keep up with the fast pace of modernization. By 1899 the Soto schools were closed, and secular, Western methods replaced the monastic approach. Many new subjects were added, such as philosophy, literature, and comparative religions. Monk's robes were replaced by modern clothing. Interaction with the West was encouraged and increased, eventually leading to Zen's voyage to the West.

Hakuin-Zen

The influence of Hakuin-Zen continued to be felt long after Hakuin died. Gasan Jito, who studied with Hakuin in the very last years of his life, had an energetic teaching style that attracted many students. Two main lines of Hakuin-Zen formed from Gasan's two main disciples, Inzan Ien and Takuju Kosen. These two branches were similar in their teaching methods and content. The main difference was in the personalities of the two leaders. Inzan was confrontational and direct, whereas Takuju was quiet and methodical. The two groups coexisted peacefully, and both flourished.

The line of Inzan passed along through five generations to Kosen Soon, Imakita Kosen (1816–92), who was the teacher of Shaku Soen, the monk who was a pioneer in opening Zen to the West.

Kosen was a forward-looking monk. He believed that the ways of Ju (Confucianism) and Butsu (Buddhism) could coexist. Taoism and Shinto should be included as well, he thought, since all is ultimately a unity. In 1862 he wrote a book, *A Wave on the Zen Sea*, as a dialogue between Confucianism and Buddhism. He also advocated academic studies, believing that they did not have to interfere with wordless insight of Zen. He did much to promote interaction with Western ideas and modernization. Kosan's student Kogaku Soen (Shaku Soen [1859–1919]) was pivotal in opening Zen to the world. His story is told in Part Two, Zen in the West: To Be One Now.

Although Japan was not the first country to receive Zen, it nourished the Zen spirit. The creative vitality of Japanese Zen was carried to the West where it was to find a renewed vigor.

CHAPTER FOUR

To Be And To Do Are Not Two: Korean Son

Korean Zen has been one of the best-kept secrets of the Orient.

—*Mu Soeng, 1987*

DURING THE T'ANG DYNASTY (A.D. 618–907), ZEN was brought to Korea directly from China's temples. Modern-day Korea now has a rich and deep tradition of Zen Buddhism, expressed in Korean as "Son" Buddhism. Korean Zen evolved distinctively apart from the Japanese and Sung Chinese forms that were based on Lin-chi's Rinzai or Dogen's Soto. The traditions that were imported to Korea in the 800s were practiced with very little interaction from outside influences. Most Korean Zen represents a line of evolution taken directly from the Zen of Bodhidharma. The mountain schools of Korean Zen, like time capsules for early Chinese Zen, kept the older traditions alive up until the Japanese occupation. Through the centuries, the clear, simple messages of the early Korean Zen masters have given Korean Zen a unique quality that still flourishes today.

•

The Three Kingdoms Receive Buddhism

Buddhism has been an important part of Korean history since the fourth century. Buddhism's influence is pervasive, reaching from the lowest peasant to the highest ruler into every facet of Korean life. The unique character of Korean Zen evolved through the contributions of certain powerful individuals who either patronized Zen or helped form and shape Korea's destiny with Zen.

In the historical era known as the Three Kingdoms period (37 B.C. – A.D. 668), all three kingdoms of the area that is now Korea—Koguryo, Paekche, and Silla—were at war with one another, attempting to exert dominance over the others as well as within their own tribes.

During this period, all three kingdoms received Buddhism. An official mission from King Fu Ch'ien (317–420) of eastern China arrived in Koguryo in A.D. 372, bringing images and scriptures of Buddhism. Paekche also received Buddhism when an Indian monk named Martar brought statues and scriptures. Silla recognized Buddhism officially in A.D. 527. The monarchs of Paekche and Silla built huge temples in the belief that this effort would bring them merit and would grant worldly success as well. The royal houses of all three kingdoms welcomed Buddhism, with its values, traditions, and worldview, hopeful that Buddhism would help each gain peace and unity.

Silla's King Chin-hung (A.D. 540–76) began an aristo-cratic academy to develop a corps of warrior knights, the *hwa rang do* (which translates as "the Flowers of Youth"), who trained in the martial arts, practiced philosophy, engaged in poetry and other literary arts, and yet held firmly to a strict code of chivalry. These knights were exemplary: inspiring to their country and unbeatable in battle. Their code became the background for the values held by modern Korea's mar-tial art, tae kwon do. Included are spiritual and ethical vows, which are integral to the art and training.

Silla was able to conquer the other two kingdoms and unify Korea (668) with the help of T'ang Chinese alliances and the hwa rang do. Korea remained unified under the Silla (668–935) and Koryu (937–1392) dynasties. China periodi-cally attempted to conquer Korea but was unsuccessful. The two countries came to a peaceful agreement known as *suzerainty,* with Korea paying tribute to China in return for China's respecting Korean borders. This peaceful coexis-tence lasted for centuries.

The Korean monk Won Hyo (617–86) was one of the most important and charismatic early influences on Korean Bud-dhism. The Won Hyo *hyung* (form) in modern tae kwon do honors his memory. Won Hyo lived freely, interacting with no-bles and commoners alike, in bars as well as in temples. He gave guidance to people wherever his presence was needed; he assumed that those who lived in poor places needed his help more than those in respectable surroundings. He was a talented scholar who lived an uninhibited "beatnik" lifestyle as part of his personal expression of enlightenment. He played a zither and drummed on an empty gourd while singing, "Only a man with no worries and fears can go straight and overcome life and death and transmigration." [1] Despite his sometimes unorthodox behavior, Won Hyo wrote more than one hundred serious works on Buddhism, twenty of which still exist today. [2] He is known as the first monk to attempt to harmonize the different themes in Buddhism, unifying them under the concept of One Mind. This was the opening wedge for Zen.

•

Zen Comes from China

The first Korean to bring Zen (Son) Buddhism to Korea was Toui (d. 825), who returned to Korea from China in the year 818. He had traveled to T'ang China during the Golden Age of Zen and spent thirty-four years studying. Toui experienced sudden enlightenment, transmitted to him by his teachers Pai-chang (720–814), Hsi-tang Chih-tsang (735–814), and Nan Chuan (748–835) without the use of words. His teachers were descendants of Ma-tsu, following his tradition.

Upon his return to Korea, Toui tried to communicate the idea of sudden enlightenment. Like his Zen masters in China, Toui developed a confrontational style of teaching. He proclaimed that what matters most is the direct pointing to the true empty nature of your mind. Toui insisted that the practice of emptiness was prior. This approach was considered heresy by the conservative and scholarly Korean Buddhist establishment, who believed that the path to enlightenment was through careful study of the famous writings and sutras. They found Toui's sudden enlightenment method shocking and argued bitterly with him. Unable to resolve these differences, Toui decided to retire from public life, moving to a remote mountain area to live and teach. There, he founded the first Mountain School of Zen Buddhism, the Kaji Mountain School. His students continued his tradition.

The Nine Mountain Schools were founded, each one on an isolated mountain in Korea.

Despite the monastic communities' reluctance to accept Zen, its simplicity captured the imagination of the people, who were tired of "state Buddhism" with its elaborate ceremonies and intellectually oriented abstract sutras. Korean Zen took root in the mountain monasteries.

During the Silla period, many Korean monks ventured to China as well as to India. Seven of the nine mountain schools were founded by monks who were direct disciples of Ma-tsu. One school was founded by a monk who learned from Yun-chu Tao-ying (dates unknown), a disciple of the founder of Soto, Tung-shan Liang-chieh (807–69). Over a relatively short period of time during the Silla dynasty period, the Nine Mountain Schools were founded, each one on an isolated mountain in Korea: Precious Forest Temple (Porim-sa), Reality Temple (Silsang-sa), Grand Peace Temple (T'ae-sn-sa), Steep Mountain Temple (Kulsan-sa), Phoenix Forest Temple (Pongnim-sa), Flourishing Peace Temple (Hung-hyong-sa), Phoenix Cliff Temple (Pongam-sa), Abode Temple (Songju-sa), and Vast Illumination Temple (Kwangjo-sa). In time there were many followers within each.

Korean Zen grew in popularity but remained independent in these remote mountain areas. Many novice monks were commoners who came from the farms. Everyday work in the fields and tending to crops became part of the religious regime. The monks raised their own food, making them self-sufficient; they did not depend on begging, though they were patronized by the country gentry families.

During the Silla dynasty, Buddhism grew to become a state religion. Monasteries flourished in the cities and in the countryside. By the time of the Koryo dynasty (936–1392), both Zen (Son) and the traditional Kyo (the Doctrinal Buddhist) schools and temples were thriving. Son and Kyo Buddhism had become deeply interwoven into the tapestry of Korean political, social, and religious life.

Korean Zen did not separate from traditional Buddhism as it did in Japan and China, where Zen temples became independent sects. It remained linked as one of the two main schools of Buddhism—the Son, or Zen Meditation School, and the Kyo, or Doctrinal Buddhist School. These years were volatile for Buddhism because of internal quarrels. The Son and Kyo Schools argued between themselves. Disagreements about theoretical positions and practices destroyed the harmony. The city temples eventually fell prey to corruption, political ambition, and petty concerns, adding to the problems.

•

Chinul: Harmony Leads to Unity

Pojo Chinul (1158–1210) was to change the disharmony and corruption facing Buddhism. Chinul cared deeply about both Zen meditation and the doctrinal schools of Buddhism. He convincingly demonstrated through philosophy and practice that Zen complemented Doctrinal Buddhism, giving it form and practicality. This unified approach has remained: in modern Korea, meditation is now integrated with Buddhist studies in the temples.

Chinul was a sickly child, born of country gentry parents. His father, fearing that Chinul would die young, vowed that if his son survived and became healthy, he would let the boy become a monk. Chinul soon became healthy and his father kept his promise. At the age of seven, Chinul was given to the monks. He received the precepts eight years later at The Steep Mountain Temple, Kulsan-sa.

Chinul taught himself from Buddhist scriptures and found them useful in refining his Zen (Son) meditation efforts. He passed the royal exam for Zen monks in 1182. He hoped to start a community (sangha) with a small group of similarly-minded idealistic monks, but although they expressed the intent, they were not willing to follow through. Chinul traveled to the south and settled on the coast.

Chinul felt committed to the lifelong quest for ever deeper enlightenment.

Upon reading the Platform Sutra and meditating on a key passage, he was awakened to another level of enlightenment. He felt committed to the lifelong quest for ever deeper enlightenment and continued to evolve through other enlightenment experiences.

Chinul was disturbed by the rift between the Zen (Son) and Kyo Schools; there was unseemly jostling for power and possessions among the monks of the city. He took it upon himself to change this situation and fight against corruption. He helped the monks renew their faith through retreats in the forests, away from the often decadent influence of king and court. There, in the sanctuary of nature, all were welcome—Zen, Taoist, Confucian, and others—and a faithful community formed around him.

Chinul introduced a concept to Korean Buddhism that is still followed in modern Korean Buddhism today: compounding sudden awakening of Son with gradual cultivation of Kyo. He thus legitimized the importance of years spent in Zen meditation and sutra studies deepening the insights. He believed that the insight from one enlightenment is only the beginning. As soon as the glow of the experience wears off, old habits automatically return. People need to change their unenlightened habits to remain in tune with the awakened state. Even though a practitioner might have a sudden enlightenment experience, he or she must learn to sustain it over time through daily practice and study, to express enlightenment in action.

Sudden awakening/gradual cultivation was Chinul's ideal, but what does this mean?

Sudden awakening/gradual cultivation was Chinul's ideal, but what does this mean? Sudden awakening is the discovery and first experience of the Buddha-mind—emptiness of all phenomena. This must be followed by cultivation of awareness in all realms of personal life, extricating oneself from defilements and entanglements to be free to help others and live a transformed life, freely expressing the Buddha-mind. The calm, thought-free mind, once realized, is then used analytically to explore and thus be liberating. This ideal permitted a synthesis between the Doctrinal and Son Schools and combined the not-thinking state with analysis from the perspective of the empty mind. The everyday practice of enlightenment deepens and makes it possible to live a noble, saintly life.

Chinul pointed out that although awakening to the realization is sudden, the maturing of insight takes time, like a child becoming an adult. Habits take time to change:

> He has the sudden awakening to the fact that his nature is originally free of defilement and he is originally in full possession of the non-outflow wisdom-nature which is no different from that of the Buddhas. . . . If thought-moment after thought-moment he continues to develop his training, then naturally he will gradually attain to hundreds of thousands of samadhis. This is the Son which has been transmitted successively in the school of Bodhidharma. Hence sudden awakening and gradual cultivation are like the two wheels of a cart; neither one can be missing. [3]

•

A Difficult Time for Zen

Japan's samurai trained in Zen and were helped by the monks, who raised money for them. In Korea, the Buddhist monasteries competed for land grants and the ruling monarchs' support. Korean monks engaged in business and were given grants of land and workers from the kings. Knights and other members of the military who expected to receive grants of land to retire to after their service frequently found that their land had been donated to the temples. Many draft-worthy youths chose to become monks to avoid military, social, and even economic obligations.

Inevitably, tensions arose as land was increasingly granted to the temples instead of to the knights who honorably served. With problems and pressures mounting, and the influence of the Mongols spreading over all of Asia, the Koryo dynasty collapsed. The Choson dynasty that followed, commonly known as the Yi dynasty (1392–1910), was Neo-Confucian and anti-Buddhist. Buddhism, associated with the earlier dynasty, was rejected and restricted. Ordination of new monks was banned and monks previously ordained were shut out of the cities and temples. Land holdings were confiscated. This anti-Buddhist, Neo-Confucian militant government attempted to obliterate Buddhism throughout Korea. The number of temples went from thousands down to a mere eighty-eight. Despite these ravages, Zen managed to live on in the remote and self-sufficient mountain temples, in the peaceful sanctuary of nature.

•

T'aego: Zen Is a Challenge

The fourteenth century saw a brief period of respite for Buddhism under King Kongmin, who attempted to reestablish the power of the Koryo dynasty. His rule ended when he was assassinated in 1374, but he did manage to unify Zen and repair many of the ravaged temples with the help of Zen monk T'aego Pou (1301–82).

T'aego was born in southern Korea. He was a renowned teacher who began his religious life as a Buddhist monk. A student of scriptures and sayings, he wandered about, temple to temple, in search of enlightenment. He meditated on koans and found the personal enlightenment he was seeking in his early thirties.

In 1346, T'aego decided to make a pilgrimage to China to study with Zen masters. He gained confirmation of his enlightenment from a master known as Shiwu, who encouraged him to go teach rather than stay. T'aego left soon thereafter and traveled to the capital of northern China where, according to legend, he taught the Mongol emperor and his court about Zen, encouraging benevolent rule.

Several years later, T'aego returned to Korea, where he tried to live in obscurity. Following a temporary weakening of the Mongol influence, the new Buddhist king, Kongmin, summoned T'aego to court to contribute his Zen expertise to ruling the country. T'aego was ordered to teach and administrate at various Zen temples around Korea. At the royal court of King Kongmin, T'aego lectured boldly, encouraging benevolent and wise rule, using Zen as a rationale and source of inspiration to the monarch. Although he would have preferred to live out his life in a mountain retreat, T'aego felt called to help reform Korea. He said, "Nevertheless, if there is anyone here with the strength to uproot mountains and the energy to top the world, let him come forward and fight alongside me. Let us sacrifice our bodies for the nation, and accomplish the great enterprise." [4]

T'aego taught techniques for koan meditation in the service of the pursuit of the deeper wisdom of enlightenment. He usually cautioned that, after achieving enlightenment, it was essential to seek out a Zen teacher to confirm the enlightenment and take the process further, as he himself had done.

The Buddhist sects continued to quarrel with each other (despite Chinul's earlier efforts), resulting in disunity and chaos. In 1356, under King Kongmin's directive, T'aego officially unified the Nine Mountain Schools into one order, the Chogye order, named for the mountain where Hui-neng had his temple. A second unification, ordered by King Sejong in 1424, melded two of the Doctrinal schools with Zen. The order was named the Sonjong. The other Doctrinal Buddhist Kyo schools were unified as one, called Kyojong.

•

Later Period

For approximately three hundred years, from the mid 1400s through the 1800s, the tides turned against Buddhism. Buddhist monks retreated to the mountain temples, where they quietly kept the traditions alive. Far away from all the urban

Zen continued in relative privacy and quiet in the mountain temples.

problems, Zen continued in relative privacy and quiet, undisturbed. The villagers and peasants of the countryside became the chief source of Zen monks. Zen doctrines and techniques of direct transmission were useful and relevant to them. Not dependent on studying scripture or literature, Zen was accessible to everyone: even poor illiterate peasants could learn.

One renowned monk of this period, Sosan Taesa (1520–1604), not only taught Zen and held a high Buddhist office but also went to jail and led a monk army.

Buddhism was repressed during the early years of Sosan's life, but in 1551 he did manage to find his way to the first monk examination offered in fifty years under a brief Buddhist revival from Regent Queen Munjong. He was given a post and a title (Todaesonsa), the highest public office in the

Buddhist hierarchy. After fulfilling his duties for a few years, he left to wander and teach more than a thousand students.

Buddhist monks were suspected in a conspiracy to overthrow the government in 1589. Sosan was accused, imprisoned, and then pardoned by the king. He returned to his teaching after being released.

Sosan was called into public duty again at the age of seventy-three when the king asked him to command a monk army to help quell the Japanese invasion of 1592. Sosan gathered five thousand monks, not an easy task on account of the scarcity of monks at the time. The monks fought valiantly side by side with Chinese armies, who were also trying to prevent Hideyosi's armies from taking over all of Asia. Sosan is remembered by Koreans for his courage and national spirit during this invasion. The following poem was composed by a Chinese army commander who fought along with Sosan in this battle:

> Caring little about worldly fame
> He had been immersed only in Zen.
> But on hearing the nation in danger
> He came down from the mountain. [5]

Sosan wrote a handbook between 1564 and 1579 for Zen students. This handbook drew together the great teachings and expressed them in commonsense language. Sosan believed that true understanding is reached without words, without thinking. A sincere effort in one's approach to meditation and koans (kong-ans, in Korean) was most important:

> To practice Zen well, you must break through the kong-an of
> Patriarchs and to realize the truth you must cut the thoughts
> away. Keep doubting without any words or thoughts.
>
> Do it as if you were always thinking of paying off your debts;
> do it as if you were a hen hatching eggs; as if you were a cat
> watching a mouse-hole . . . . The practice of Zen requires
> dogged determination in order to succeed. [6]

Following Sosan Taesa, most Zen monks remained in
their mountain temples, quietly teaching Zen to those close
by but having little effect on the Confucian, anti-Buddhist government. Buddhist monks were officially banned from entering the cities. This law remained in force for three hundred
years. It was not until the Japanese pressured the Choson government that this restriction was finally removed in 1907.

The Japanese colonial rule (1910–45) did not prove positive for Zen. Periodically the Japanese tried to force Korean
Buddhists to merge with Japanese Soto. These efforts were
not successful, and certain Japanese influences caused disputes among Korean Buddhists.

One of the most threatening was the push by the
Japanese to allow Korean monks to marry. Some Korean
monks felt this to be a positive step toward modernizing.
One spokesman for this position, Yongon (1879–1944),
championed a movement to bring Buddhism out of its isola-
tion. He was the first Korean to encourage interaction
with the West. His advocation of monks' marrying found little support within the Buddhist order. Despite Korean

objections, Japan instituted a married clergy, which divided Korean monks into two groups: married and celibate.

By 1953, after the Korean War, Korea began to reach back to its earlier roots to rediscover national pride and Korean character. President Syngman Rhee ordered all "Japanized monks" to be replaced by celibate monks. [7] The married monks refused to comply. Confrontation ensued through the Korean courts. The matter was finally resolved in 1962 when two separate orders were established. The celibate monks formed the Chogye-Chong, using the traditional name from the Koryo and Choson dynasties. The married monks, who traced their lineage back to T'aego Pou, formed the T'aego-Chong. Today the Chogye-Chong order is dominant in Korea but the other orders, though smaller and less powerful, continue separately.

In the twentieth century, Zen reemerged from the sanctuary of the hills through the writings, lectures, and teachings of many great Zen masters. They carried on the classic traditions, reintroducing Korean Zen to the people. One master named Mang Gong (1872–1946) opened his monastery doors to everyone. He taught: "All of you are monks. Monks are free of petty personal attachments and live only to serve." [8] His teachings were transmitted to Seung Sahn, who came to America, adding the seeds of Korean Zen to American soil.

Korean Son, with its roots in Ch'an from T'ang China, made its mark on the Zen spirit, unifying meditation with Buddhist studies and sudden enlightenment with gradual cultivation.

For thousands of years the spirit of Zen swept through many countries in the East, transformed by every culture it encountered and transforming those who embraced it. Zen was to find new life—journeying across the sea to the West.

ZEN
in the WEST:
TO BE
ONE NOW

ZEN HAS BEEN TRANSMITTED TO AMERICA AND Europe. It continues to grow and evolve, yet it remains intimately connected to its roots in the East. Modern movements from dynamic Japanese, Korean, and Western masters express the spirit of enlightenment that was transmitted from teacher to student since its legendary beginning. Now Zen has been welcomed in the West.

Art, sports, political activism, and psychotherapy have been influenced by and integrated with Zen. Modern Zen continues to blossom in every corner of contemporary life. The seeds of the future are now.

CHAPTER FIVE

TRANSITIONS

•

D. T. Suzuki Introduces Zen to the West

The West and East coexisted as two separate worlds of meaning for centuries. With the exception of some individual interaction between the two cultures, little exchange took
place until the end of the nineteenth century. This changed
in 1893 when a worldwide conference on religion was held
in Chicago. Many Eastern religious leaders presented
philosophies that spurred great cross-cultural interest. Zen
was represented by Shaku Soen, a disciple from the line of
Hakuin, who spoke English poorly. An insightful Japanese
Rinzai master, he had the foresight to bring Daisetsu Teitaro
(D. T.) Suzuki (1870–1966) as translator. Through this conference, Suzuki met with an American publisher, Paul Carus
(1852–1919), founder of the Carus Publishing House, to
translate a series of Eastern writings, beginning with the
Tao te Ching. Suzuki remained with Carus, living at his house

in Illinois for ten years (1897–1908) while he wrote and translated books on Zen and Taoism. Suzuki became one of the most important emissaries of Zen to the West. He opened a whole new perspective to the Western mind. His translations drew from original works written in Sanskrit, Pali, Chinese, and Japanese to give his writings authentic depth. Educated in European studies and fluent in English, German, and French, as well as Chinese and Japanese, Suzuki returned to Japan to teach Buddhist philosophy at Gakushu-in University in 1910. The following year, he met and married an American woman, Beatrice Erskine Lane (d. 1939), who shared his broad religious perspective, and returned with her to Europe and then on to America. In his later years, after World War II, Suzuki made an extensive lecture tour across America and even taught college courses at Columbia University in New York City. Through his prolific lectures, writing, and teaching, Suzuki spread Zen wisdom across America.

Suzuki was not just an academic scholar but also a devout Buddhist. He studied Zen under Rinzai Master Imakita Kosen (1816–92). According to Christmas Humphreys, who was one of his students and a writer and teacher of Zen in London, Suzuki was honored at many temples in Japan.

Over his long and productive life (he died at the age of ninety-five), Suzuki wrote over 125 books and articles in English and eighteen books in Japanese. At home in both Eastern and Western cultures, Suzuki was able to communicate Zen so that Westerners could not only understand it conceptually but also identify with it and embrace it. He inspired lasting interest in Zen, with its promise for wisdom and spiritual fulfillment through satori.

Suzuki's approach to Zen came from Hakuin's Rinzai tradition, although he reinterpreted it to be more understandable to the Western mind. He often used Lao-tzu's Taoism to illustrate Zen concepts of enlightenment. Hakuin benefited from Taoist healing visualizations, and taught simple methods to his students to help them. Suzuki also used Taoism.

Suzuki traced the history of Zen through Hui-neng and believed that the Sixth Patriarch's approach to Zen could be considered the beginning of Zen as we know it today. As Suzuki expressed it:

> From the first "not a thing is"—this was the first exclamation made by Hui-neng. It was a bomb thrown into the camp of Shen-hsiu and his predecessors. By it Hui-neng's Zen came to be sharply outlined against the background of the dust-brushing type of Zen meditation. [1]

Suzuki was a mystic. He believed that there is a way of perceiving through "prajna intuition," a different way of perceiving that is much more accurate and closer to truth than logic and reason. Suzuki was opening to Westerners the possibility for greater wisdom through their own experience. The mystical side of Zen, satori, draws upon intuitive insight; it is not unlike the mystical experiences pointed out by William James in his *Varieties of Religious Experience*, a book Suzuki studied and liked. [2] People encounter enlightenment with a feeling of exaltation, release, an infinite expansion of their own individuality. Suzuki believed that enlightenment comes about abruptly, all of a sudden. In fact, he said, if it is not abrupt and momentary, it is not satori. [3]

Suzuki likened the Zen state to the unconscious mind, but he was always careful to clarify that he did not intend this to be a psychological interpretation of the unconscious; rather, he was referring to the *nonrational* quality of mind. When talking about enlightenment, he communicated with intensity, immediacy, and sincerity, beyond reason and language.

Suzuki's work spanned every aspect of Zen practice. He explicitly described daily life in a Zen monastery. He clearly depicted the use of koans as an integral part of Zen. He translated many of the significant sutras that influenced the Chinese masters. He also translated the significant koans based upon the experiences of the T'ang and Sung masters. Truly, Suzuki brought the seeds of Zen that now bloom in the Western mind.

•

Zen Masters Bring Zen to America
Rinzai Travels West

Several Japanese Zen masters, all disciples of Soen, the monk who attended the World Conference in Chicago in 1893, openly shared their wisdom with the world. Tetsuo Sokatsu (1870–1954) traveled to Thailand and Burma, and spent a short time in California. His disciple Sasaki Shigetsu (Sokei-an, 1882–1945) opened the First Zen Institute of America in New York City in 1930, where Ruth Fuller Sasaki served as director for many years.

Nyogen Senzaki (1876–1958) first came to the United States when he accompanied his teacher Soen to San Francisco in 1905. Senzaki decided to stay in California after his teacher left. As the first Zen master to come to America, he found California of the early 1900s an open highway for Zen, which was then virtually unknown to any Westerner. Out of nothingness he created "floating zendos" in rented halls where he began to teach Zen. He tried to make his teachings accessible to Americans. He spoke in English as well as he could. Students did zazen on folding chairs, since he thought that sitting cross-legged on the floor seemed un-American. In 1931 he moved to Los Angeles and opened a modest but stable Mentogarten Zendo, as he called it. He offered a quiet style of Zen, "too square for Beat Zen." As he said, "I have neither an aggressive spirit of propaganda nor an attractive personality to draw crowds." [4] Despite his quiet ways, his sincere style drew a number of serious students to him. He taught them that when they learned to quiet their minds, a spiritual dimension would be revealed. His clear, simple approach allowed his American students to savor the Zen spirit.

With financial help from his American students, Senzaki brought Nakagawa Soen (1907–84) to America. Versed in Western philosophy, Nakagawa Soen was known for his creative melding of both traditions, useful during this period of transition. When Buddhism was brought from India to China, it was integrated with Chinese culture, traditions, and philosophy. Similarly, the early Japanese Zen masters who came to America often presented their teachings through Western culture and thought. For example, Nakagawa ended his New York retreats with listening to Beethoven symphonies. He would say, "We in truth can know nothing," but went on to explain that this paradox was what Zen was all about: the study of the unthinkable. When his mother became ill in 1962, Nakagawa returned to Japan to care for her. He arranged for Hakuin Yasutani (1885–1973) to take his place in America.

Yasutani's training included both Soto and Rinzai. He gave his American students no special treatment, subjecting them to the same strict discipline and often combative tactics as he had given his students back in Japan. Each student underwent probing individualized questioning that helped bring them beyond conceptual thinking to enlightenment. His teachings became known through the popular book written by Roshi Philip Kapleau, *The Three Pillars of Zen.* Yasutani, as one of Kapleau's teachers, was a great pillar of Zen, touching Westerners with his dynamic style of teaching.

Many Westerners devoted themselves wholeheartedly to the lessons from the enthusiastic emissaries who brought Zen to the West. Today, Americans and Europeans have become masters who write and teach, transforming the spirit of Zen.

Shunryu Suzuki Brings Soto

There was another Suzuki who had a profound effect on Zen in America, Shunryu Suzuki (1905–71). A monk in the direct succession from Soto Zen Master Dogen, Shunryu Suzuki was a very different sort of person from D. T. Suzuki. Small and quiet, his lifestyle reflected his life's way, the Soto Way of non-ego. Despite his subtle manner, he left an indelible mark by establishing the first Soto Zen monastery in the West, the Zen Mountain Center in Tassajara, California, and the San Francisco Zen Center.

Shunryu Suzuki's Zen was different from that of D. T. Suzuki. He never emphasized satori or enlightenment. Zen, he felt, should not be pointed toward an ecstatic experience. Rather, it should involve concentration on everyday, regular routines. Keep your mind calm and constant and over time your character builds. He explained it as follows:

> Buddha also said that building character is like building a dam. You should be very careful in making the bank. If you try to do it all at once, water will leak from it. Make the bank carefully and you will end up with a fine dam for the reservoir. [5]

Shunryu Suzuki taught that the purpose of studying Zen Buddhism is to study ourselves. Buddhism might guide you along the way, but ultimately *you* are the Buddha, and the learning takes place within you. Dogen said that to study Buddhism is to study ourselves. Suzuki took it one step further by stating that to study ourselves is to forget ourselves. When we forget ourselves, we can become one with the greater universe. Shunryu Suzuki clarified Dogen's thought:

> When we forget ourselves, we actually are the true activity of the big existence, or reality itself. When we realize this fact, there is no problem whatsoever in this world, and we can

enjoy our life without feeling any difficulties. The purpose of our practice is to be aware of this fact. [6]

Through practice of meditation—or "concentration," as Suzuki called it—people experience true freedom. How we find this freedom is by just sitting. He often told people that it was enough just to sit.

Through practice of meditation people experience true freedom.

Suzuki felt positive about Americans. He saw great potential in their openness to ever flowing moment-to-moment reality, or "beginner mind," as he called it. He devoted himself to his Zen teaching, quietly, calmly just being himself. His legacy included an active, vital Zen Center in America and growing interest in the calm, quiet Soto Way of Zen.

Korean Son Comes to America

Korean Zen found its way to the West through a trickle of Korean Zen Budddhists, but the open-minded Zen master, Seung Sahn (b. 1927) was primary. He spent many years devoted to the Choyge-Chong order, the Korean Buddhist organization. But when he heard in the early 1970s that there were many "wild-spirited hippies" in America who were open and searching, he decided to bring Korean Son to the United States. He had no money and spoke no English when he first arrived in Providence, Rhode Island. Some students from Brown University heard about this interesting monk from Korea and came to his tiny apartment to study. From this embryonic beginning, the Kwam Um School of Zen developed into a thriving center for Zen studies.

Seung Sahn made changes in roles, customs, and rituals

to adapt Zen to America. In traditional Korean Zen, women cannot become dharma masters, nor can they receive transmission. In America, in keeping with the freedom and equality inherent in the American culture, Seung Sahn has allowed women to receive transmission as equals and wear the robes of a monk, and he allows families to meditate together. All may practice regardless of life circumstances: Christians, Buddhists, Jews, young, old, rich, poor, working men or women. This is in the classic tradition of Zen, yet in harmony with *now*. Through these changes, the experience of enlightenment continues to be transmitted without hindrance.

The fundamental state of consciousness for this approach to Zen is "Don't-know mind." Koans (kong-ans, in Korean Zen), chanting, question and answer, and sitting meditation can all bring the Zen devotee to the realization that not to know is the beginning of knowledge. Searching deeply within begins the process. Openness of mind becomes possible when people don't know. When they are already filled with their own ideas, opinions, and judgments, they are not open to receiving. The first step, therefore, is to admit that you don't know.

Seung Sahn exhorts students to sincerely devote themselves to Zen. "Only go straight," he likes to say. Do not waver or wobble. People must follow the path they are on without distraction. There is great discipline involved in Zen meditative life. Give one hundred percent to your efforts. If you are a contractor, be fully that; if a psychologist, be fully that. If a martial artist, be fully committed to what you do. Find your center, your direction for your life, and just do it! Do not

**Not dependent on words,
A special transmission
ouside the sutras.
Pointing directly to mind,
See your true nature,
become Buddha.**

−Zen master Seung Sahn

focus on results. Keep your correct situation moment to moment. If hindrances arise, says Seung Sahn, "Put it all down."

In the twentieth century, the pioneers traveling from the East found many eager Americans who opened their hearts sincerely to Zen. Today, generations are sharing their wisdom with new generations to keep the spirit of Zen ever evolving. Westerners and Easterners have united in spirit to help Zen thrive. The roots reach back from India to China, Korea, and Japan while the branches now flourish and spread across America and around the world, blooming like cherry blossoms in the spring.

•

The Dogen Revival

Dogen has been remembered as the founder of the Soto School and the main proponent of the value of sitting in zazen meditation. However, he was forgotten by most people outside of the Soto sect. In the 1920s, a well-respected professor at Imperial University in Tokyo, Watsuji Tetsuro, wrote a long essay on the significance of Dogen's work. [7] He showed how Dogen offered universal truths, that Dogen's work was relevant for all humanity. For the first time, many people, both Eastern and Western, took note. The Kyoto School agreed with Watsuji's view and many essays and analyses followed throughout Japanese intellectual circles.

The Dogen Revival was underway. As his popularity grew, dozens of books about Dogen were published. In 1981 a Dogen conference was held in California, at which his relevance and importance for modern Westerners were discussed.

observe themselves and experience themselves as existing separately from the world. The Eastern idea of the self is that it exists as part of the larger universal "all." The self is not the stream of consciousness but exists as something prior to consciousness. Nishitani thought that Descartes realized this in his famous conclusion, "I think, therefore I am." He had experienced a breakthrough like Zen enlightenment. He speculates that Descartes named his book *The Meditations* to indicate that he was pointing to an experience different from normal, rational thought. [10] From his own Eastern perspective, Nishitani thought that Descartes went astray when he tried to use his intuitive breakthrough as a basis for rational reason.

Today, scholars continue in the Kyoto School tradition of bridging the gap between East and West through Zen. Always the efforts have been to tackle the important human problems that affect our contemporary age. Zen masters past and present offer alternatives that are relevant as long as human beings continue to search for fulfillment of the human spirit.

•

Westerners Who Taught and Wrote Zen

D. T. Suzuki's books and the early pioneers touched many in the West who began thinking about Zen and integrating it into their own spiritual experience. A few of the early contributors are presented below as examples of some varied ways that Westerners began teaching and writing about Zen.

Christmas Humphreys, a British leader in the introduction of Buddhism to the West, taught classes in Zen for more than thirty years. He was integral to the London Buddhist Society from its inception. He also served as D. T. Suzuki's London agent, helping publish a dozen of Suzuki's books.

Humphreys recognized the great spiritual potential that Zen has to offer Westerners. He often told people that the East does not have a monopoly on the Zen experience. He recognized that the expression of Zen would be altered by the Western mind, just as it had gone through changes in China, Korea, and Japan. However, he felt certain that with mind training, Westerners can experience the true Zen spirit.

He taught people to let go of fixed assumptions, stop thinking, and start meditating. Meditation to him was not simply an emptying of the mind but a method of developing an entirely new way of dealing with things. Meditation is with us throughout our day as we live. "Living life as life lives itself," [11] enjoying each moment, busy, happy, and always fully aware.

R. H. Blyth was another Westerner who contributed greatly to the introduction of Zen to the West in the 1950s and 1960s, with five volumes devoted to Zen and the Zen classics, four books on haiku, and books comparing Zen to literature. He felt that the real threat to our modern age was the growing trend toward mechanistic and "unpoetical" lifestyles. He firmly believed that the study of Zen would help people rekindle a deeper, spiritual sense of life. Zen could be compatible with Western ideas. As he said, "'Man is the measure of all things' has its parallel in the Buddhist idea that without man there is no Buddha." [12] He hoped to make it possible to find an integration that could include "[both] the

Buddha in eternal peace, and the Christ in eternal agony." [13]

Eugen Herrigel (d. 1955), a German professor of philosophy at the University of Tokyo, was an early Western proponent of Zen. He and his wife, Gustie (1887–1974),
attempted to penetrate deeply into the Zen experience by
subjecting themselves to rigorous training with Zen masters
for six years. Eugen studied archery and his wife learned
flower arranging. Both brought their experiences to the West
through uniquely personal accounts: *Zen in the Art of Archery*
and *Zen in the Art of Flower Arrangement.*

Through Zen, life can be lived as an art.

Both Herrigels learned that, through Zen, life can be
lived as an art, wherein everything we do, even the most mundane, expresses that art. Eugen practiced the state of purposeless detachment, of emptiness with each drawing of the
bow. He felt confused at first, but after many years he said to
his master:

> "Bow, arrow, goal and ego, all melt into one another, so that
> I can no longer separate them. For as soon as I take the bow
> and shoot, everything becomes so clear and straightforward
> and ridiculously simple . . ."
>
> "Now at last," the Master broke in, "the bow-string has
> cut right through you." [14]

Gustie explained how Zen art becomes life itself:

> . . . the pupil should realize with his entire being the "unwrit-
> ten teaching" until it becomes second nature to him, mould-
> ing his character until he can go the "flowers' way" in his own

life here and now. Then all groping ceases: the way has become living reality. [15]

Ruth Fuller Sasaki was one of the first American women to become an ordained Zen Buddhist priest. She was brought up in a strict Presbyterian family, but turned to the study of Buddhism in her early twenties. At the age of forty she practiced under Rinzai master Nanshinken of the Nanzen-ji monastery in Kyoto and later with Sokei-an Roshi (Sasaki Shigetsu), whom she married. She wrote several books on Zen and helped found the First Zen Institute of America in 1930 with her husband. Back in Japan, she continued her studies with Goto Zuigan Roshi. She set up a small Zen research center in her home while living in Kyoto. Professor Iriya Yoshitaka, Kyoto University; Professor Seizan, Hanazono College; Philip Yampolsky, Columbia University; Gary Snyder, the Beat poet now at University of California, Davis; and Burton Watson, Columbia University made up the group. All have continued to write and teach about Zen.

Another woman who helped enhance Western understanding of Zen was Nancy Wilson Ross. She was born in the Pacific Northwest and made her first trip to Japan, Korea, and China in 1939. Throughout her life she traveled extensively to the East, writing articles and books on many Eastern topics. She also served on the board of the Asia Society of New York City.

Alan Watts, who held a master's degree in theology and a doctorate of divinity, was a creative thinker who did much to help integrate Eastern and Western thought. He lectured and wrote over twenty books through the 1950s and 1960s. Watts's books became widely read, helping people to make links with areas such as psychotherapy and philosophy, as well as religion. His interest was not merely in importing Zen from the East but in inspiring Westerners to learn or "unlearn from it and apply it in our own way." [16] Watts's creative perspective and clear, commonsense manner of expression did much to help Zen make the transition from East to West.

•

Zen and Christianity

Early in this century, a number of Christian scholars and monks became fascinated with the points of convergence between Zen and Christianity. Their inspirational enthusiasm also did much to introduce the Zen spirit to the West.

Germany learned about Zen in the early twentieth century through a renowned philosopher of religion, Rudolf Otto, who was one of the early European thinkers to grasp the Zen spirit. He wrote the introduction to a German translation of a collection of classical Zen texts entitled *Zen: Living Buddhism in Japan* (1925) and wrote other essays comparing Zen to Western mysticism. His understanding was clearly stated in one of his essays in which he asked an aging abbot at a Tokyo monastery what was the fundamental idea of Zen. The abbot answered him by explaining Buddhist philosophy. Otto realized that what he was really saying was that Zen is not fundamentally an idea but rather an experience.

As a religious thinker, Otto had great respect for the ferocity of the Zen quest, as depicted by the burning intensity in Bodhidharma's eyes. He believed this single-mindedness led to an opening of "one's heavenly eye." [17]

Otto's broad understanding of religious mysticism helped him put Zen into a context that Westerners could begin to grasp, opening the doorway to integration between East and West.

Christian theologians viewed Zen as an alternate perspective of the religious experience.

Hugo Makibi Enomiya-La Salle (1898–1990), a German Jesuit, spent twenty years learning and practicing Zen. Once he felt that he had mastered Zen well enough to share it with others, he began teaching in Germany in 1968. His class, "Zen Meditation for Christians," made Zen accessible to Westerners. Many Europeans attended the classes taught by La Salle and others. Students found that the straightforward methods of Zen meditation enriched their lives and added a new dimension to the Christian experience.

Dom Aelred Graham, prior of a Benedictine community in Rhode Island, thought searchingly about the religious significance of Zen and attempted an early, sometimes critical, analysis in his book *Zen Catholicism*. Graham believed that much of Zen is suited for Catholic practice. Graham retired in 1967 to learn more and continue his spiritual quest. He traveled throughout India and Thailand, engaging in dialogues with learned Hindus and Buddhists, seeking the ultimate grounds of religion. He spoke with many types of people, from anonymous abbots of Buddhist and Hindu monasteries to the president of India! Graham's search led him to include Christianity, Zen, and Hinduism in a synthesis that transcended any one religion.

> By thus enlarging and purifying our consciousness, we
> learn to see life from the standpoint of total existence
> and accordingly to know the truth that makes us free. [18]

Graham taught that the message of emptiness in Zen ultimately creates a hopeful openness with great potential. Shared meaningful experiences without words become possible. The awakened one also feels identity with and compassion for others who are still stuck in the quagmire of worldly concerns and illusions. This is similar to the sentiment of *agape* (Christian love).

Thomas Merton (1915–68), a Trappist monk who delved into Zen to deepen his commitment as a monk, devoted himself to exploring and teaching about the relationship between Zen and Christianity. He was deeply influenced by Dom Graham's thought, even carrying Graham's books with him on his own journeys to the East. Merton had fruitful dialogues of his own with D. T. Suzuki and many others, including the Dalai Lama, who gave him some guidance and instruction.

Merton saw parallels between Zen Buddhism and the early Christian mystics through meditation and the vows, such as humility, silence, and simplicity, practiced by all monks. He believed that Zen meditation could help one rediscover purity of heart and viewed the emptiness of Zen enlightenment as a way to recover the innocence of paradise lost. Herein lies the beginning of a spiritual quest.

From its origin in India, Buddhism spread to China and was influenced by Taoism, the native religion. Zen evolved and continued on its journey. In Japan, Zen integrated with

Japanese Shingon, Confucianism, and Tendai. Upon its arrival in the West, it has intrigued Christians everywhere. Where it will lead, we may not yet know, but we can be certain that the dialogue between Zen and Christianity will continue.

•

The Parliament of World Religions (1893 and 1993)

The Parliament of World Religions in 1893 forever changed the religious exchange between East and West. One hundred years later, in 1993, eight thousand people from more than 125 countries gathered together in Chicago to celebrate the centennial of that monumental meeting. All types of diverse religions were represented, with participants interacting and attending over two hundred lectures and seminars offered each day for nine days. Having come full circle, participants from East to West freely exchanged ideas and shared together in the silence of meditation and prayer. What had only a century ago seemed foreign and strange now was accepted and enjoyed together as one.

•

Contemporary Zen

Today Zen has found a home in cities around the world. From Los Angeles to New York, London to Berlin, the Zen spirit offers inspiration and renewal. As in historic China, Korea, and Japan, Zen also continues to be practiced in mountain retreats and remote country areas.

Zen in the West is Zen from the traditions of Soto and Rinzai, in varied combinations or emphases depending upon the sect. Some schools are devoted to the study of Soto Zen, such as the San Francisco school started by Shunryu Suzuki. Others have remained true to the Rinzai tradition, such as the First Zen Center of New York, founded by Sokei-an, under the guidance of Ruth Fuller Sasaki, and the New York Zendo under Eido T. Shimano. There is also a contemporary movement to integrate Soto and Rinzai, as taught by the many dharma heirs of Maezumi Roshi, including Dennis Genpo Merzel, Bernard Tetsugen Glassman, and John Daido Loori.

Zen can be adapted to be useful in modern times. Like water, it takes the form of the vessel that contains it without any change in its nature: water remains water whether it is held in a rice bowl or in a coffee mug. Many who seek enlightenment in this day and age may not be able to fulfill their destiny within a purely monastic lifestyle. Modern Zen practitioners are learning to live their Zen as they work at jobs and take care of the mundane needs of life, to keep the balance of giving and receiving. At the same time they pursue enlightenment through both active practice and formal meditation.

In early Japan, Korea, and China, lay monks had a different role from the monks who devoted their entire lives to the monastery. Modern Zen continues this tradition by offering varying types of involvement: as a monk in a monastery or a student at a Zen center. Joining a monastery as a monk becomes a full-time commitment with a distinct structure and a set of clearly defined practices, rituals, and precepts. A Zen center, on the other hand, offers the option of remaining part of worldly life: one can contribute from earnings outside, attend morning and evening meditation practice, and participate in group life and retreats. The decision to live in a center involves a second step of commitment, one that distinguishes Zen center life from everyday life at home. Some may even prefer to stay with their own lifestyle, to have a personal and individualized experience of their own, outside of a monastery or Zen center.

Modern Zen organizations offer Americans an opportunity to learn Zen at different levels of involvement.

Modern Zen organizations offer Americans an opportunity to learn Zen at different levels of involvement. Most Zen centers periodically hold lectures, workshops, and retreats that can last from a single day to several months. Retreats give participants an opportunity to focus on inner development. Through meditation, chanting, and question-and-answer sessions, people get a direct experience of Zen. Even meals and caretaking of the premises are approached with a Zen spirit. Some centers have expanded their activities to include instruction in related arts, such as martial arts, Chinese painting, and spontaneous poetry guidance. All these options are available to open the doorway to the Zen experience. Ultimately, Zen is beyond words, beyond time, beyond place. How you discover the Zen spirit must come from within.

> The great path has no gates,
> Thousands of roads enter it.
> When one passes through this gateless gate
> He walks freely between heaven and earth. [19]

•

Women in Zen

Traditionally Zen was thought of as a patriarchy, with men in the dominant positions. However, women have been involved in Zen throughout its history, though their contributions have gone unrecorded. Today egalitarian involvement of both men and women is growing in the West. Many women have made contributions and received recognition as a matter of course.

Barbara Rhodes has been designated as the dharma heir of the Kwan Um School of Zen by Korean Zen Master Seung Sahn. This is an unusual occurence in the East but it is becoming more common in the West.

Maura "Soshin" O'Halloran, a young Irish-American woman who was tragically killed in a bus accident in Thailand in 1982, left a legacy through her journal of her training (1979–82) at Toshoji Temple in Tokyo and Kannonji Temple in Iwate Prefecture, Japan, under Roshi Tetsugyu Ban. She said in one entry:

> The place is totally non-sexist. I half expected to be pointed towards the kitchen, but I saw wood and move furniture with the best of them. And no condescending "Didn't she do well?" It's just taken for granted. I'm totally "one of the lads," except I'm not bald. [20]

Eventually she did shave her head and received *Denpo-shiki,* transmission ceremony. The true message of Zen, when it is practiced at its best, is, There is no woman; there is no man.

Having made the journey to the West, the Zen spirit began to take root and grow. New developments, unique to the Western mind, would inevitably find their expression through Zen.

CHAPTER SIX

The Beats:
On *the* Road *to*
Enlightenment

What's your road, man?—holyboy road, madman road,
rainbow road, guppy road, any road, it's an anywhere
road for anybody anyhow.

—Jack Kerouac

THE BEATS WERE A GROUP OF INDIVIDUALS IN THE
1950s who took their inspiration from America's élan vital,
excitement about life, and combined it with their own interpretation of Zen. Allen Ginsberg, Jack Kerouac, Lawrence
Ferlingetti, Neal Cassady, Gary Snyder, and William S. Burroughs were among the more well known.

Dogen wrote that without commitment to the Buddhist
precepts, there is no Zen. Traditional Zen, he felt, must include a vow to these higher values. The Rinzai curriculum included Confucian values as well as the Mahayana sutras to
guide conduct. Every action and ritual of life was carefully
specified by the masters. Zen Buddhists believe that they

must live according to these absolute values on the one hand, yet hold no relative value sacred on the ultimate level: enlightenment is neither relative nor ultimate.

The Beats interpreted Zen to mean freedom: freedom from convention, from rules, from restriction; freedom from what was perceived by them as stuffy, prudish, and inhibiting. The Beats held no conduct sacred. They believed that they could find enlightenment through ecstatically losing themselves in intense experience, whether that be stimulating action or just traveling as a religious experience. Mountain climbing, driving fast cars, drinking, sex—any of these activities might be used by Beats as a path to enlightenment. They perceived the enlightened life as an invitation to live freely. By doing what they wanted without inhibition, they hoped to find ecstatic enlightenment.

The Beats interpreted Zen to mean freedom.

> Yessir, that's what, a series of monasteries for fellows to go and monastrate and meditate in, we can have groups of shacks up in the Sierras or the High Cascades or even Ray says down in Mexico and have big wild gangs of pure holy men getting together to drink and talk and pray, think of the waves of salvation can flow out of nights like that, and finally have women too, wives, small huts with religious families, like the old days of the Puritans. [1]

The Beats, in their best moments, were uninhibited, spontaneous, jazzlike in their abandon to life, "digging" experience. As a consequence, they were not always true to traditional Zen values: social boundaries became constricting to them.

Kerouac claimed that *Beat* stood for "beatitude," a holiness sought in everyday life. In their lifestyle the Beats attempted to express this philosophy of spontaneous action with detachment. The hipster idealized cool detachment in action. The more emotionally stimulating the action, the more the Beats sought to be "cool," challenging the boundaries with paradox.

> In his most enlightened state, the hipster feels that argument, violence and concern for attachments are ultimately Square, and he says, "Yes man, yes!" to the Buddhist principle that most human miseries arise from these emotions. [2]

The Beats combined their interpretation of the Buddhist concept of detachment (emotional detachment) with a search for excitement, for "kicks," in the enjoyment of everyday life. This was parallel to Zen, but without formal practice under a master and without commitment to the precepts. To the Beats, ordinary life in America was their sangha. Kerouac considered the common person a saint.

Though they engaged in conduct that "square," or mainstream, society disapproved of and found troublesome at times, their enthusiasm for life and other people was wonderfully refreshing. Their intent was to live an enlightened life through immersion in ecstatic actions and experiences while cultivating, paradoxically, detachment: "coolness."

Kerouac developed a theory of Beat artistic composition: spontaneous, literary expression. This approach dramatically affected the poetry, literature, and other artistic composition of the Beats. Creative individualistic expression was freed and enhanced along with the spontaneous vitality of the artist. Kerouac believed that writing should be spontaneous and free from literary devices, flowing from the pen as naturally as speaking. He wrote in the everyday vernacular, without formal, stylized grammar. He hoped to express the Beat vision and inspire his readers with enthusiasm for it with his deliberate approach to spontaneous expression in writing. His style may better be described as "stream of expression" than stream of consciousness. Kerouac developed consciousness through engaging in action. Unfortunately, some of these very actions became personally problematic. The source of enlightenment needed renewal again, but the Beat vision transcended personal interpretation, as a great universal vision always does, on the road to fulfillment.

The Zen Beats were seekers who had not yet found. Zen helped them to be creative. Beat Zen was an American derivation of classic Zen adapted to the lifestyles and creative endeavors of artists, painters, writers, and jazz musicians. It became a phenomenon that was carried abroad to Europe and other countries as well. Yet Beat Zen needed to be modified to regain contact with a deeper wellspring of holiness.

Thirty-five years later, many of the Beats are still productive and creative. Beat methods of creativity continue to evolve. Allen Ginsberg taught his spontaneous methods of poetic creation. Gary Snyder is a professor of literature and poetry. Others still write, create, or perform—with more seasoned wisdom and without the mistakes of excess and

negative habits acquired on their earlier path to enlightenment.

Kerouac, who popularized the Beat perspective, died
tragically early from health conditions aggravated by
overindulgence in alcohol and drugs. Ginsberg died of liver
cancer later in life. Many Beats were drawn into drug use in
an attempt to enhance their perception and consciousness,
but they eventually found it limiting. Ginsberg said, "Well,
the Asian experience kind of got me out of the corner I
painted myself in with drugs." [3] Burroughs, a Beat writer of
fiction, also found drugs to be detrimental:

Beats found meditation was the superior route to expanded perception.

> The hallucinogens produce visionary states, sort of, but mor-
> phine and its derivatives decrease awareness of inner
> processes, thoughts and feelings. They are pain killers, pure
> and simple. They are absolutely contraindicated for creative
> work, and I include in the lot alcohol, morphine, barbitu-
> rates, tranquilizers—the whole spectrum of sedative drugs. [4]

Once the minds of the Beats had been awakened to their
visionary capacities and their consciousness explored, they recognized that meditation expanded their perception far more
than drugs possibly could. Meditation is the superior route.

> . . . Poetry, poetic practice is sort of like an independent car-
> pentry that goes on by itself. I think, probably, the meditation
> experience just made me more and more aware of the hu-
> mor of the fact that breath is the basis of poetry and song—
> it's so important in it as a measure. [5]

New concepts and ideas arise when those concepts long-cherished and held sacred are let go. When there is nothing, there can be a something. Creative artists cannot be bound only to the known.

> That was always a basic principle, to write a poem by not writing a poem. . . . Things I didn't expect were important, turned out to be the best poetry, because the spontaneous mind was more straightforward, full of strong detail. [6]

Zen lent itself to application by many of the Beats, who found much in Zen to guide them in creative expression while living the Beat life. However, Zen need never be limited to any one lifestyle. In fact, Zen can be usefully adapted and applied to enhance many facets of living.

CHAPTER SEVEN

MIND OVER MATTER: ZEN ARTS

The sunyata of Buddhism is not the emptiness of absence, it is not a nothing existing beside a something, it is not a separate existence, nor does it mean extinction. It is always with individual objects, always coexistent with form, and where there is not form there is no emptiness, "Form is emptiness and emptiness is form."

—*D. T. Suzuki*

ARTS LIKE FLOWER ARRANGING, THE TEA CEREMONY (also known as Teaism), martial arts, haiku poetry, calligraphy, Noh drama, and many others have been imbued with the Zen spirit. Zen arts are a process through which the artist and his or her creation become one. By sensitive meditative awareness while creating, the Zen artist remains mindful and gives this mindfulness to the creative process.

The inner richness of Zen is brought into the outer world through art. All who share in the artistic experience can be enriched. The art speaks for itself to the beholders. If they are also mindfully aware, they can receive a glimpse of transmission through communion with the mind of the artist during direct experience of the work itself.

The Zen arts have much in common. They are all "Ways," that is, *paths* to inner development. If the practitioner takes the art seriously and practices it with harmonious wholeness of body, mind, and soul, a transformation inevitably takes place.

Zen arts offer a "way" or "path" to inner development.

To practice a Zen art you must learn to empty yourself of any petty disturbances, of all ego, to become "carefree as a flower of the field." [1] This comes about through the rigorous discipline of following the traditions of the art absolutely. At first, resistance or distractibility may arise. Gradually, with the passage of years devoted to practice, the art begins to sink in to the bones, becoming one with the artist. Then something original emerges, from the inner wellsprings of the creative Zen genius, the Buddha-mind latent in us all.

•

Cha-no-yu: The Art of Tea

Imagine that you are walking though a beautiful garden. With each step you notice plants carefully arranged. You feel as though each step takes you farther and farther away from the clamor of the outside world. Fragrant aromas tantalize your senses as you walk along a stone path. You come to a water basin, set low. You kneel down to carefully wash your hands and face in the crystal clear water. Feeling cleansed and somehow humbled, you arise and continue along the path. Just ahead you see an unpretentious thatched wooden structure standing by itself. You duck down to enter through a low doorway. The diffuse light softly illuminates a calligraphic scroll hanging by itself on a wall. A flower in perfect bloom rests in a stoneware vase on the floor. As you enter the room and notice a tea kettle sitting on a fire pit, you hear water bubbling. The master enters, carrying several simple utensils. He bows quietly and sits; you bow and sit down on the mat with him. He begins to prepare the tea, moving effortlessly yet precisely, wiping the bowl dry with a clean linen napkin, ladling in water, spooning the tea, stirring it carefully. A meditative silence pervades the room. Subdued sounds of clinking and tapping gently massage your senses. You find your attention turning inward, yet you are also becoming intensely, fully aware. All is in harmony with the surroundings. The master offers you a cup of tea. You are surprised and delighted by the delicate, subtle taste. You feel renewed, completely at peace with yourself and the world.

The spirit of tea embodies what Zen is.

This is the tea ceremony, cha-no-yu, an ancient tradition that has carried the Zen spirit to the modern day. The spirit of tea embodies what Zen is: the philosophy of tea is the philosophy of emptiness. Just as Zen aims to strip away all things artificial, so a tea ceremony helps people return to the ultimate ground of being, at one with nature, lucid, fully in the moment.

Tea was originally used by the monks in China to chase away sleep during long hours of meditation. Later, during the Sung period, tea became part of the monks' rituals, used to produce a peaceful calm. Some ritual ceremony was attached to tea drinking. The Chinese developed a method of pulverizing the young tea leaves and then whisking them with a brush, an integral part of the traditional Japanese tea ceremony today.

Eisai, the first Japanese credited with bringing Zen from China to Japan, also brought Chinese tea plants and methods of tea drinking with him. He sowed the *kanime-gata* seeds on the grounds of his temple and wrote two informative volumes explaining everything he had learned about tea. When the local shogun became ill, Eisai brought him tea to help speed healing. The shogun recovered so quickly that he credited his cure to tea. The healing powers of tea were widely promoted, partly as a result of this incident.

At the temple, Eisai's student Myozen cultivated a flourishing tea garden, grown from Eisai's original plants. This particular strain of tea still exists, having been perpetuated for centuries. Today it is known as *honcha* or original tea.

A significant change in the nature of the tea ceremony was effected by Mokichi Shuko (1453–1502). He became the first to find his Zen enlightenment through tea and become recognized as a Zen tea master. While he was a Zen student, he found himself continually falling asleep. His teacher, Master Ikkyu Sojun (1394–1481), suggested that Shuko seek help from a physician. The doctor prescribed tea, so Shuko began drinking tea often. Soon he invited other people to join him in a tea ceremony he performed for guests. Everyone enjoyed the occasion, and word spread of these wonderful, peaceful ceremonies. Shogun Ashikaga Yoshimitsu, a great patron of Zen Buddhism, heard about Shuko's teas and invited him to present a formal ceremony to him personally. The shogun liked it so much that he gave Shuko a rustic hut where he could devote himself full-time to tea. Shuko realized that tea drinking was one with the Buddha Way, the Way of Zen. Master Ikkyu gave Shuko his Dharma Seal, making him the first ordained Zen tea master.

Shuko introduced a special atmosphere for the tea ceremony: quiet space, solemn beauty, and perfect imperfection are the path to the tea Way. He encouraged the Japanese to stop admiring the refined style of Chinese utensils and create their own simpler, more natural tools. Eventually Japanese craftsmen, who were also followers of the Way, created Japanese pottery. Each piece was made with a small deliberate imperfection to symbolize the human, handmade quality and the limits of human will in the face of the universe. During this period, plain Korean pottery crafted anonymously also grew in popularity as representative of these values of simplicity and imperfection. Nothing was allowed to intrude on the simple purity. The teahouse was simple, poor, natural, and inconspicuous—nothing to disturb the tranquillity of the heart.

Sen no Rikyu (1521–91) was the founder of the Tea Way that is practiced today. As is characteristic of Zen in general, Rikyu asserted that tea was nothing special. When a student asked him to reveal the deeper secrets of tea, he answered:

Tea is naught but this,

First you make the water boil

Then infuse the tea

Then you drink it properly

That is all you need to know. [2]

The student thought this was a superficial answer and said sadly, "I already know that!" The master responded, "If there is anyone who knows it already, I should like very much to become his pupil!" He went on to explain, "It is similar to what the Chinese masters said many centuries ago: 'Don't do any evil. Instead practice every kind of virtue.' This is something every child of three knows, but a philosopher of eighty cannot carry out!" Upon hearing this, the student was enlightened.

Rikyu believed that tea was a way of life and embodied certain virtues common to both Zen and tea: reverence, harmony, purity, and tranquillity. Harmony includes gentleness of spirit, which springs from deep inner compassion for all beings and is central to Zen as well. When Dogen came back from China, people asked him what he had learned. He said, "Oh, not much except soft-heartedness." The implication of this seemingly small learning is profound, since it leads to a spiritual outlook on everything in life. Reverence is respect for others and also self-control of the ego. Purity refers to orderliness, not just with the use of tea utensils and tea rituals but in every act of life. Tranquillity draws from the Zen principle of emptiness. Rikyu said:

The water that fills the kettle is drawn from the well of the mind whose bottom knows no depths, and the emptiness which is conceptually liable to be mistaken for sheer nothingness is in fact the reservoir of infinite possibilities. [3]

At its very heart, tea is a "quiet simplicity *(wabi)* and a mellow experienced taste *(sabi)*." [4] The Japanese terms *wabi* and *sabi* point to the way to approach tea: be unconcerned about fashions of society, power, and reputation and yet feel an inward presence of something that has more value. Like Thoreau's log cabin at Walden Pond, the teahouse and tea ceremony embody the virtue of simplicity. With wabi one learns to be self-sufficient, even with an insufficiency of things. Those who know wabi are free from emotional out-bursts, greed, and frivolous pursuits. If wabi refers to doing with less, sabi relates to what we do have. Our belongings should be aged and ripe with the patina of experience. With sabi we feel deep solitude, even loneliness, yet profound peace.

> When you take a sip
>
> From the bowl of powdered Tea
>
> There within it lies
>
> Clear reflected in its depths
>
> Blue of sky and gray of sea. [5]

•

Ikebana: The Art of Flower Arranging

Where better than in a flower, sweet in its

unconsciousness, fragrant because of its silence, can we

imagine the unfolding of a virgin soul? [6]

The Japanese Zen art of flower arranging (*ikebana* in Japanese) is another school of experience where mere technique is not the essence; practicing with the heart is what counts. As with tea, there is a rigorous disciplining of the mind through ritualized technique that brings about a change within. Both women and men practice this art.

Flower arranging is associated with certain virtues that mirror Zen. Masters carry nothing in mind. They are empty, quiet, and clear, without thought. They practice self-denial and reserve, always trying to be free from evil. An intimate, sensitive relationship with plants, with nature, nourishes the soul. Flower arranging can bring about a profound religious feeling.

The relationship between flower arranging and Zen virtues is not merely a theoretical connection but an active, living link. Intertwined with the process itself, philosophical concepts are expressed in the placement of every blossom, every branch.

Sensitivity to the plant's true nature comes from more than a momentary interaction; it also derives from having the right attitude toward nature in general. An old legend explains this relationship. A young girl came to her local well to draw water, only to discover that a trailing vine had wound itself around the rope that pulled the bucket. Basking in the early yellow sunlight, a single blossom had opened itself to the day. The girl delighted in its beauty for a few moments. Then, so that she would not disturb the plant, she walked out of her way to the next well, where she happily drew her water. A haiku poem was written to celebrate this Zen relationship between human being and nature:

Round my well-rope

Wound a convolvulus

Give me water, friend. [7]

The primary virtue—union with the "flower heart"—begins from the very first moment spent with the flowers. Flower arrangements are created without speaking, in a meditative, focused state of mind. A bundle of flowers is untied with care. Thoughtfully, the flower artist chooses the branches to be used, sensing the potential harmony of the flowers together. The artist enters into a reciprocal relationship with the plant as each branch is carefully felt to determine where it wishes to bend and twist. These natural inclinations are put into the arrangement. Lost in the moment, the flower artist adapts patiently and unobtrusively to what is given by the flowers' tendencies. Ego is unimportant. Listening with the sense of touch, the flower artist turns his or her whole being to the flowers as they are tugged and pulled gently into patterns. Together as one, the nature of the flowers and of the arranger is expressed. Through the meditative state the connection is made.

Japanese flower arranging embodies Zen emptiness. In the same way that the masters tried to express things in very few words, flower arrangements must be simple, almost spartan. Equal attention is given to the open spaces and the branches themselves in the design. Arrangements are made in patterns of three: one branch reaches for heaven, one for the earth, one for human beings in the middle. Though arrangements might become more complex, the pattern remains true to form.

The outward form is merely a bridge leading to the inner essence. Thus, the choice for the arrangement is esteemed most highly when it "draws the eye inwards to the depths where nature and spirit, life and ideal are one." [8] As the unity between artist and nature unfolds over time, truth takes a visible form. The Zen art of flower arrangement, like all the Zen arts, embodies the Zen spirit in our world and brings it to full flower.

•

Haiku: The Zen Art of Poetry

Haiku is the expression of a temporary enlightenment in which we see into the life of things. [9]

Japanese haiku poetry is another art that has found expression through Zen. Haiku unifies what is outside us with what is inside our mind. There is no division between subject and object. The essence of things is best understood when perceived directly, without thought.

The mushroom:

from an unknown tree a leaf

sticks to it. [10]

Bashō (1643–94), who was known as the First Pillar of Haiku, was one of the greatest Zen haiku poets. Haiku was the way he expressed his Zen understanding; he created a haiku as a result of his enlightenment. He was studying Zen under Buccho, who asked him, "How are you doing these days?"

Bashō answered, "Since the last rain the moss is greener than ever."

Buccho probed deeper. "What Buddhism is there even before the moss has grown greener?"

Bashō answered, "A frog jumps into the water and then the sound." Eventually he created this haiku:

Haiku is simply what is happening in this place at this time.

> The old pond,
>
> A frog jumps in:
>
> Plop! [11]

Bashō explained that haiku is simply what is happening in this place at this time. As in Zen, you must stay with your "now" experience, fully aware in the moment. This profound level of mind is often awakened by nature, as Bashō expressed in his poems. Bashō lived Zen through his art, merging himself with nature and expressing it poetically.

> On a withered branch
>
> a crow has settled . . .
>
> autumn nightfall. [12]

The traditional Japanese rules for haiku are simple: a seventeen-syllable poem with three lines. In modern haiku the rhythms that fit the Japanese language may deviate in translation, and thus modern adaptations may not adhere to the strictest form. But despite these creative variations, haiku is always unadorned and stripped-down.

This concept of using only a few, well-chosen words is similar to the idea of sparsity in flower arranging, or the economy of cha-no-yu, also known as the tea ceremony. As Suzuki said, "Haiku is not rich in ideas, speculations, or images. Haiku is loneliness itself." [13] What is actually being expressed is the Zen virtue of simplicity, that the answers to life's deepest questions are so simple that most people miss them. Haiku is about everyday experiences, things that are often overlooked. As Blyth said, "Nothing is little to him who feels it with great sensibility." [14] Although the small things in life may seem insignificant, they become "precious treasures and inexhaustible riches to anyone who has learned not only to look but to see." [15]

In haiku, some reference to nature is made expressing a particular event occurring in the present. Haiku has been described as "a record of a moment of emotion in which human nature is somehow linked to all nature." [16] The haiku poet tries to re-create the circumstances that aroused this deeper, intuitive insight. The circumstance is presented so that readers can experience the same feeling that the author felt: a moment of a human life experiencing nature. Emotion is rarely described—this is left to the reader. Listening to haiku read aloud or reading it to yourself provides a glimpse of transmission of mind: haiku communicates the experience—a quality shared by all Zen arts.

Haiku has become very popular in America. As early as the 1960s there were many people writing haiku in English.

In 1964, the Japanese Air Lines National Haiku Contest attracted forty-one thousand entries. The best haiku captured many of the qualities of the ancient poets, while some used modern images. One first-place haiku calls forth an American national symbol:

> Searching on the wind,
> The hawk's cry . . .
> is the shape of its beak. [17]

Another winner:

> Lily:
> out of the water . . .
> out of itself. [18]

The Beat poets also experimented with this art form, attracted by its immediacy and stark directness. Blyth shows how haiku and Zen can be one:

> A haiku is not a poem, it is not literature; it is a hand beckoning, a door half-opened, a mirror wiped clean. It is a way of returning to nature, our moon nature, our cherry blossom nature, our falling leaf nature, in short to our Buddha nature. [19]

•

The Art of Noh Drama

There are many who have long frequented the theater, but do not understand Noh; and many who understand, though they have little experience. For eye-knowledge comes not to all who see, but to him who sees well. [20]

Noh is the Japanese art of drama. *Noh* means "to be able." About the thirteenth century in Japan, acrobats and jugglers entertained in small troupes. By the fourteenth century, Noh performances had evolved into theatrical operas and dances. Actors danced and sang and sometimes "mimed" the action while a chorus sang the words. As time passed, dramatic performances added rhythmic sounds, chanting, and movement. Frequently the dance was preceded by narration that described what the play was all about.

Noh drama makes use of the interplay between emptiness and fullness.

One Japanese family line in the fourteenth century was most influential in shaping the form of Noh dramas: the Buddhist priest Kwanami Kiyotsugo (1333–84), his son Seami (1363–1444), and their descendants. When Shogun Ashikaga Yoshimitsu (the same shogun who became involved with tea) attended Kwanami's Noh drama, he was impressed and decided to foster the Noh art.

Noh drama makes use of the interplay between emptiness and fullness by manipulating everything—sets, costumes, music—as they intertwine with the plot. Audiences watch a minimally decorated stage set behind an elaborately costumed and masked actor. Background music is sparse, a few notes from a flute with long silences interrupted by the sharp catlike cries of the chorus and eerie use of the human voice. The plays can last as long as six hours, with a preset program including five interrelated plays about gods, followed by plays about a warrior, a woman, a madman, and finally, devils. The deeper meaning behind the play's action draws from Zen philosophy.

The actors harmonize with the mood of the spectators. If a gloom comes over the audience, the actors respond by performing with more positive energy to uplift them. Voice, silence, motion, stillness, ghostly apparitions, and tangible, vital, emotional players alternate and complement one another.

Seami took over after his father's death, creating more than ninety plays. Seami often used simple elements to stir deeper emotions in his audiences, such as a sudden sound, a long silence, an artistically placed foot movement. Not only an actor and playwright, Seami also wrote about Noh drama, laying down exacting rules and specific suggestions to guide writing and acting for Noh dramas. [21] One of the most famous, *Sotoba Komachi*, written by Seami's father, Kwanami Kiyotsugo, is still performed today.

Noh was popular with the samurai class, who could relate to the Buddhist ideals that were portrayed. More than eight hundred Noh plays have survived; most were written before the seventeenth century. Noh drama was resurrected in the late 1890s after the restoration of the monarchy.

Noh has been directly and indirectly linked to Zen Buddhism. Noh plays partake of the qualities of all Zen arts. The dramas provide an experience that enchants while invoking the meaning of Zen through stories of personal tragedy, or Buddhist redemption through enlightenment's release from the bonds of the self, with its illusions, impulses, and conflicts. The once beautiful and now ugly tragic heroine, Komachi, of the Noh drama *Sotoba Komachi,* experiences the pain and suffering she had caused her lover as she dies. Her enlightenment that comes with her death is echoed in the words of the chorus:

> See I offer my flower to Buddha,
> I hold it in both hands.
> Oh may He lead me into the Path of Truth,
> Into the Path of Truth. [22]

Often, some of the most poignant Noh passages occur when the actor wordlessly communicates through mime and gestures.

> The *Book of Criticism* says, "Forget the theater and look at the Noh. Forget the Noh and look at the actor. Forget the actor and look at the 'idea.' Forget the 'idea' and you will understand the Noh." [23]

•

Zen and Martial Arts

Zen is karate; karate is true Zen. [24]

In Japan, Zen has been intimately linked with swordfighting and the samurai class since feudal times. Today, karate, fencing, tae kwon do, kung fu, and other martial arts draw technique and inspiration from Zen.

Swordsmen

Takuan (1573–1645) was an exemplary Rinzai Zen monk who had a profound influence on martial arts philosophy. His unusual talents were recognized early. He became an abbot at Daitoku-ji in Kyoto at the youthful age of thirty-five. He inspired two generations of shoguns and samurai in his own time, including the renowned swordsman Myamoto Musashi. He was also close friends with Yagyu, master of the School of the Sword of Mystery. Takuan's writings included discussions of Zen in general as well as specific applications of Zen to swordsmanship. He believed that the mind should be allowed to roam freely throughout the body without being fixed in one place. The mind must not be concentrated in any particular limb or part. This permits one's responses in combat to be highly attuned, without distraction from extraneous thought that might be delusional. Response time is quick, since there is no gap between thought and action. Similarly, the Zen attitude aims to be clear-minded, open, and direct. The Zen-oriented martial artist must not allow attention to be fixed in any one place. Mind should not be restrained, since this can lead to rigidity: forced, narrowed attention creates problems. The sphere of attention should be widened so that total immersion in the moment becomes possible.

The technique of swordfighting is affected by this manner of using the mind. In the midst of battle, sword and opponent become one. There is no gap or interval of any kind. Nothing exists. The swordsman has no enemy. There need be no fear, no guilt, no concern. He has no doubts or questions of judgment. In the ultimate comprehension, there is nothing to judge and nothing to understand. There is no way to conceptualize what is taking place: wisdom in combat is not a product of analytical thought or of reflection. It derives from sensitivity and perception. Thus, no strategy for combat is necessary, since direct attunement is more effective. The ultimate technique becomes no technique; like a flash of lightning, the encounter ends as it begins. Actions can thus be performed faster, with total commitment and dedication, guided by Zen instead of by conceptual strategy.

Zen Focus in Martial Arts

Martial arts can be divided into two classifications: those that are for sport or are tournament-oriented, and traditional or classical arts. Many of today's traditional styles continue to draw from Zen as part of their curriculum, teaching it directly through meditation training during practice. But apart from this relationship, there is a deeper connection, one implicit within the martial arts themselves. Those martial arts that are tournament-oriented arts do not partake of this aspect.

Zen's doctrines add a profound spiritual character to everything that the traditionally-oriented martial arts student does in practice.

Zen's doctrines add a profound spiritual character to everything that the traditionally-oriented martial arts student does in practice. Complete absorption in patterns of moves, intense awareness of the body in motion, and full immersion in the action—these are the outer manifestations of the inner character of Zen. Tae kwon do, as currently taught by Grandmaster Duk Sung Son and his instructors, continues this approach. Duk Sung Son's style directly encourages One-ness without ever labeling or conceptualizing it as such. In-stead, he teaches by example, with few words and strong actions. "Always best!" he shouts, inspiring rows of students to put every ounce of energy and concentration into each movement. The class radiates Oneness with dynamic mo-mentum, a characteristic of Son's approach.

Mas Oyama (1928–93), founder of the Kyokushin style of karate, pointed out that there is need for the intense con-centration of Zen when attempting to accomplish great things in life. High levels of achievement are possible even in seemingly non-Zen fields through devoting oneself entirely to the activity, whether it's the laboratory for scientists, the building site for architects, the university for students, or the office for businesspeople.

Often his Western karate students complained that Zen was too difficult for them. He countered confidently that far from being difficult, Zen can be practiced by anyone, any-where. "How?" they would ask. He answered:

> Right now go through some karate techniques with a sincere mind and intentions and with total mental unification. If you do this, the opponent will cease to exist for you, there will be no more distinction between enemy and ally, and winning and losing will become unimportant. You will have suc-ceeded in entering a Zen state. [25]

He believed that everything people do can be Zen if they are in a clear-minded state of Oneness, fully identified with what they are doing. In this way, all activities can be opportunities to enter the Zen state.

Mind/Body Unity through Martial Arts

Martial artists seem to be doing the impossible when they break stacks of wood or bricks without injury. This skill not only draws on the physical techniques learned in martial arts but also requires exceptional development of mind. Breaking techniques are used in many martial arts to test a practitioner's mental and physical skills. Breaking requires complete presence in the moment, without holding back. If the practitioner is uncertain at the moment of the strike and does not follow through, the break cannot be accomplished. Hesitation, doubt, lack of focus—all can contribute to failure. A secondary aspect to breaking is the willingness to try again if the practitioner does not succeed the first time. Usually, the striking point of the martial artist hurts after a failed first attempt. Yet another attempt may be called for, until a successful break results. Technique is important, as is proper conditioning, but these alone will not result in a successful board break without the unified mind, body, and spirit of the practitioner being brought into focus at the moment of the strike.

The martial arts instructor presents material to learn with a strict set of procedures, rituals, and movements. The instructor expects students' attention to be intensely concentrated on what they are doing. They are expected to perform all movements with focus. In practical terms, this means that all movement must be performed thoughtlessly, with awareness, speed, power, focus, balance, and accuracy. All the practitioner's available attention must be trained on the action. Wandering thoughts and actions are discouraged. The instructor calls out a command to perform a movement, and the entire class responds strongly, as a unit: Oneness. Naive observers note this as discipline, but a deeper analysis shows that the class manifests the spirit and intensity of meditation in action. Martial arts demonstrates that Zen meditation can be far from passive and quiet!

Forms provide an excellent test for the unity of concentration and meditation. Forms are like the literature of martial arts, passed along from teacher to student. Each form contains attack-and-defense patterns that are practiced and perfected. If the martial artist is distracted, the form movements may lose their crispness, their vitality, and even the proper sequence of details of movements can be misperformed, to the detriment and embarrassment of the martial artist. Forms require intense absorption in the moments of action to have the quality expected.

Upper-level practitioners must show their comprehension at a deeper level, not just a superficial memorizing of a movement or self-defense sequence. The movements suggest many possible applications, concepts, and principles. When applied in this way, forms become the martial arts equivalent of the Rinzai approach to a koan. Okinawan systems of martial arts such as Goju Ryu, founded by Chojun Miyagi, developed this extensively.

In other systems, such as the World Tae Kwon Do Association, forms are not analyzed but are used instead as foci of concentration to develop reflexes and understanding that remain more on the unconscious levels. The practitioner uses them more for conditioning and intense awareness.

In one modern innovation known as *tae chun do,* practitioners use the forms both analytically and as focal points for meditation. Unconscious reflex patterns later become manifest as ideas, and concepts of movement as solutions to problem situations. For example, when the practitioner is sparring, techniques implicit in the forms are available spontaneously, drawn from the deeper reservoir of the mind. This meditative approach combines the best of both the Rinzai and Soto schools. The practitioner is tested and evaluated in terms of the depth of intense, unified, empty-thought as well as the inner meanings of the movements.

Tae chun do combines meditation with martial art technique.

After some years of involvement in the martial arts, a subtle change takes place in practitioners. They find themselves guiding actions in their lives with the strategies and constructs of the martial arts. Intensity, full commitment, and whole-heartedness translate into humility, respect, honor, and discipline. These virtues generalize to other significant relationships in life. Advanced-level martial artists are respectful to others, disciplined in important endeavors, and humble where appropriate as a natural development of their maturity. The Zen monk's everyday humble, respectful, and disciplined manner is similar.

•

Zen and Sports

The art of effortless concentration is invaluable in whatever
you set your mind to. [26]

The goal of inner approaches to sport is to use focused concentrated mind and to be fully unified with what you are doing. Learnings apply to all aspects of your endeavors. The
concentrated mind is one with what the body is doing. Everything works together automatically without interference
from thoughts about the actions.

Timothy Gallway's popular approach called the Inner
Game of Tennis applied Zen and Eastern approaches to
tennis. Many other applications suggest themselves. Zen
guides people to become more in tune with the tennis experience. Watch the tennis ball as an aesthetic object in motion.
Seek for fascination; listen to the ball; watch its pattern, its
trajectory. The sound of the ball when hit is different, depending on where in the racquet it hits, what the shot is, fore-
hand or backhand, and so on. Ask your body to do what is
necessary to reproduce the sound.

The "trick" in Zen applications to sports—whether tennis,
golf, or archery—is to get one's ego out of the equation: be
one with the interaction without judgment or rational involvement. As Gallway wrote, a racquet is not always where it
should be in a stroke but it is always where it is. Therefore, it
is more effective to stay focused simply on what is moment-to-
moment with the swing, fully attentive and oriented to its position. Your emotions during the game, attitudes, worries,
and anticipations are not the central point of attention. It is

more important to stay with the primary events, the action itself: tennis is activity, your body and the ball in harmony. The swing, ball, and racquet must be a unity. Your body has the resources. You only need to let it happen.

When you concentrate on the moment-to-moment details of how you act in any sport, your problems dissolve. Your body and mind work together to automatically and naturally perform well. You do not need to strive for a goal: the action works on its own when performed this way. People think of achievement, of goal-directedness, as vital, but if they simply allow awareness, everything happens naturally and better and they reach their goals without even trying!

So I must become purposeless on purpose. [27]

Mastery of form brings mastery of mind. The Zen arts point toward enlightenment. Person, technique, and goal become one. Transcending technique is the ultimate expression of the art. Great skill appears, but no one can claim the credit. There is no opponent, no contest, no technique. All dissolve in the sea of Oneness. Art leads from the periphery to the center. The center is the interaction, the relationship of person, art, and action. Archery, flower arrangement, haiku, tea, martial arts, tennis, running, and even daily work, when approached in this way, become an art that expresses the Buddha-mind.

To Be Is *to* Act: Zen Activism

THE FOUR GREAT VOWS TAKEN BY MAHAYANA MONKS, including Zen Buddhists, include the vow "Sentient beings are numberless, I vow to save them." The other three vows are:

The passions are inexhaustible, I vow to extinguish them.
The dharmas are immeasurable, I vow to master them.
The truth of the Buddha is incomparable, I vow to attain it. [1]

The practice of enlightenment is not just for ourselves but for all beings. In order to realize enlightenment fully, Zen Buddhists bring the practice of their vows into everyday life. This has been interpreted in many ways.

Some Zen Buddhist groups have taken Zen's philosophy to mean that they should enter into the realm of activism. They believe that to take action is a logical extension of Zen practice, carried forth into daily life. There have been many

Zen Buddhists who have felt that their situation calls them to try to do something to help others here and now. They interpret this to mean social and political action for causes that they value.

As Korean Zen Master Seung Sahn has said to his followers:

> Great love and compassion is not something to do for the sake of doing good. Great love and compassion is not a thing to do for the sake of doing a good deed. Great love and compassion is our original job. So I hope all of the people in this world can find their correct and original job, get enlightenment, and save all people from suffering. [2]

•

Activism for Peace

In Cambodia a group of Buddhist monks, including Zen monks under the leadership of the Venerable Preah Samdeach Maha Ghosananda, has been actively trying to bring about peace in the minds of the Cambodian people. They have undertaken many activities to make their ideas felt. On May 3, 1993, the monks gathered a group of four hundred monks, nuns, and laypeople to march for sixteen days across the war-torn country. The concept of walking for peace is as old as Buddha himself, who would take large processions of followers marching across the countryside and teaching peace. The Venerable Maha Ghosananda's message for peace in Cambodia is intended to speak for peace worldwide: "Our journey for peace begins today and every day . . .

The concept of walking for peace is as old as Buddha.

slowly, slowly, step by step. Each step is a prayer. Each step will build a bridge." [3]

Thich Nhat Hanh, a native of Vietnam, is a man who has dedicated his life to the struggle for peace and has applied the concepts of Zen Buddhism to political action. He has often said that his work has followed the Buddhist precept of not harming any living creature—everyone and everything has Buddha-nature. To make this principle a reality, he feels that people must all learn to practice nonviolence to some degree. He recognizes that no one can be completely nonviolent: even monks who boil their drinking water may be killing microorganisms and thereby doing violence. Although no one may be completely free of violence, everyone can learn to be less violent. Therefore, he preaches to army generals on both sides, encouraging them to moderate their strategies by not killing innocent bystanders. He exhorts his followers not to hate the other side but rather to approach all with love. The struggle for peace ultimately comes back to ourselves and learning to deal peacefully within.

If we nourish mindfulness every day and water the seeds of peace in ourselves and those around us, we have a good chance to prevent the next war and diffuse the next crisis. [4]

Healing the scars left by war and hate comes through meditation. Gradually the elements of war within us are transformed.

In the practice of mindfulness, we nurture the ability to

see deeply into the nature of things and people and the fruit is insight, understanding, and love. [5]

He urges people to start with moderation. Even one minute of breathing in and out calmly may begin a process of change that leads to a less violent mind and thus less violent reactions.

Thich Nhat Hanh has found that meditation helped him time and time again. He tells how one time his meditation helped him rescue eight hundred people. In 1976 he had been involved with the plight of the boat people in the Gulf of Siam who were sent back out to sea to starve, rejected by the governments of Thailand, Malaysia, and Singapore. Just as he was about to work out amnesty for them, word of his work leaked out to the press. The Singapore authorities served him deportation papers, giving him only twenty-four hours before he must leave the country. The night before he was to be deported, he was overcome with anxiety and worry. He paced and ruminated, lamenting the fact that he would not have enough time to finish the arrangements and that the poor boat people were surely doomed to death. The more he tried to think of a solution, the more upset he became.

Then he remembered a meditation topic, "If you want peace, peace is with you immediately." [6] Calmly and quietly he focused and gathered himself inwardly. He meditated through the night, becoming calmer and clearer until suddenly, spontaneously, a solution that would resolve the difficulty appeared before his mind—to ask the French embassy

Thich Nhat Hanh has found that meditation has helped him to help others.

to extend his visa a few days. The extension was granted, giving him enough time to save these eight hundred lives. Only in meditation was he able to clear away obstructions so that solutions could arise. The power to be able to find peace, even in the midst of crisis or danger, is the power Zen meditation can give.

The work of Thich Nhat Hanh has brought the plight of many to the attention of the world. He worked tirelessly to help bring an end to the Vietnam War, asking governments and veterans to help bring about peaceful changes in the world. He has written about saving the planet based upon Buddhist principles. He calls it "meditation on interbeing endlessly interwoven." [7] Ultimately, he believes people must realize their interdependence with all that makes up our world and then find peace within. Zen meditation puts us on the Path to find the Way.

•

Activism for the Environment

Buddhists, including Zen Buddhists, believe all beings have Buddha-nature: people, animals, and plants. Thus, all things and all people should be treated with respect. This belief has led some Buddhists to work in the area of ecology. In 1990 the Global Forum of Parliamentary and Spiritual Leaders for Human Survival brought religious leaders together with political leaders to discuss humankind's relationship to the world. One of the key issues raised was how human beings may be destroying the world, and what can be done to prevent it.

The question of what our relationship to the environment is has been carefully addressed by Shakyamuni Buddha's teachings. He explained that our life springs not merely from our parents. The earth, water, air, and sun all help to support our life as well. Therefore, people not only have an obligation to their own parents for bringing them into the world, they also have an obligation to all the elements of the earth for sustaining them.

Zen traditions encourage ecological living.

Zen Buddhism encourages people to develop awareness of their place in nature. One example is the "Born as the Earth Intensive" retreat sponsored by the Mountain and Rivers Order in Mount Tremper, New York. Participants spend five days immersed in nature. By becoming more aware of their environment, the participants grow to feel a deep connection with the world. From such awareness, a transformation can take place.

In Zen monasteries, there is as little waste as possible. Eating ceremonies encourage people to take only the amount of food they will eat and to be certain to eat everything in their bowls. Scraps, peels, and any other waste are saved in a bag and used for compost to fertilize the garden. These traditions, though often very ancient, encourage ecological living.

Nuclear waste is a daunting problem that threatens our environment and seems to have no solution. The Nuclear Guardian Project has used meditation's mindfulness to help. Joanna Macy, an activist in this area, suggests that instead of ignoring the situation, people should pay very close attention to the storage of nuclear waste and carefully watch it over time. This will prevent accidents before they happen. [8]

The vast ecological problems facing Earth seem overwhelming. Many of us despair of solving them; many of us become aggressively angry. Zen offers a different, calmer perspective. The solution begins within each person. We are capable, through meditation, of emptying our minds of doubt, despair, and anger. Doubts, fears, and hopelessness about the problem only make it doubly difficult to resolve. If we all have a clear mind and commit ourselves to improving the environment, the situation cannot help but get better.

In the spirit of the tea master Rikyu, who said "Don't do any evil; instead, practice every kind of virtue," Zen Buddhists learn to allow the inner Buddha-nature that is within to manifest in action. When thought, feeling, and behavior are one, Buddha-nature is expressed.

For Zen Buddhists, attaining enlightenment is only the beginning. It is important to be aware, moment to moment, of what you are doing. When you are aware in the moment, you care about and respond to suffering in the world. The Zen spirit reaches out, beyond self-centered individual interests, with concern for the welfare of others. We are all part of the Oneness, including suffering beings. Their suffering is our suffering. The enlightened response of Zen Buddhism is compassion.

CHAPTER NINE

BEING WHOLE:
ZEN *and*
PSYCHOTHERAPY

From ancient times physicians have sought a panacea, a medicina catholica, and their persistent efforts have unconsciously brought them nearer to the central ideas of the religion and philosophy of the East.

—Carl Gustav Jung

CARL GUSTAV JUNG (1875–1961), RENOWNED pioneer of psychotherapy, explored Eastern religions despite the aura of mystery surrounding these philosophies. At the end of his life he was immersed in studies of the *I Ching,* a classic Chinese work of antiquity. He found great value in this and other Eastern writings for Western psychotherapy. In the 1960s and 1970s, Zen was applied to psychotherapy, though it had to be modified and compounded with certain standard therapy methods to be used with patients. Certain theoretical approaches permitted Zen to integrate well with psychotherapy.

•

Field Theory

A new approach to conceptualizing, known as field theory, drawn from advances in theoretical physics, was adapted and developed by the Gestalt psychologists to revolutionize psychology. This was the opening wedge that began the movement to embrace and westernize these Eastern approaches.

Field theory holds that an interaction always takes place as a whole. The individual components or elements of an interaction form a compound, a field that is more than just the sum of its parts. The individual elements are always interacting, and are therefore interdependent. Any division into its separate elements is artificial and ignores their necessary unity in what is occuring. All interactions take place as a whole and must be understood as a field, not just as a combination of individual elements.

All interactions take place as a whole.

An analogy helps explain field theory. A molecule of water will represent the interaction. Water is a liquid with the formula H_2O. Although the molecule contains both hydrogen and oxygen, it has qualities that are more than just those of its constituent gases, because it is a compound. Take any of its constituent parts away and it ceases to be. Similarly, a car, though it consists of an engine, a set of wheels, seats, a windshield, and numerous other parts, is more than just those parts alone: it is a unity as a car, with all the possible functions that a car can perform when the parts all work together as a system. A car can be a means of transportation, which its engine or even its seats could not do alone, in and of themselves, without the interaction with all the parts of the car as a unity. The car requires all parts to work together before it can become a means of transportation. Many of us have experienced this when some essential part of our car stops working or is broken and we cannot get where we need to go. The unity consists of interdependent parts but is not limited to them. This is field theory in action.

Eastern approaches are similar. For example, Nagarjuna's theory is a field theory view of reality: all the parts are codependent and nonexistent individually, to form the field, the emptiness.

•

Gestalt Therapy

Gestalt therapy, founded by Frederick Perls (1893–1970), drew from field theory to develop a method of psychotherapy. Based in the present, the here and now, and in the centerpoint, or the zero point, the nothingness, Perls conceptualized that all of us mature throughout our lives, becoming the unique individuals that it is our potential to be. He called this self-actualization. Problems arise when our true nature is obstructed somehow, our natural tendencies unnaturally inhibited and prevented from full expression. As a consequence, rather than evolving and maturing, we adjust and remain stuck at an inappropriate level of development.

Perls's theory of Gestalt therapy revolved around the central axis of nothingness.

> In our culture "nothingness" has a different meaning than it has in the Eastern religions. When we say "nothingness,"

there is a void, an emptiness, something deathlike. When the Eastern person says "nothingness," he calls it *no thingness*— there are no *things* there. There is only process, happening. . . . And we find when we accept and enter this nothingness, the void, then the desert starts to bloom. . . . The sterile void becomes the fertile void. [1]

Nothingness is the ultimate truth, the criterion. Explanations and theories—all are illusions. Process, no thingness, is central to reality, and experiencing it is fundamental to cure. Perls worked with patients in therapy to help them come to the point of their troubling impasse through the experience and acceptance of nothingness. He believed that most people fear the void, nothingness. When they enter the void, they find that the void is not just empty. It is filled, pregnant with possibility. Suddenly the patient wakes up to awareness of how he or she is stuck. Then growth, release, and transcendence become possible. New potential emerges. Perls called this a "mini-satori." [2]

Perls sometimes drew from Zen meditation technique when he performed therapy. He presented a statement to his patients to contemplate as a koan: nothing exists except the Now. He believed that it sometimes took years for people to grasp the meaning of this koan. By focusing attention on what is here and now, successful therapy can take place. Whatever you do, whatever you experience, he would say, you do it now. If you remember the past, you remember it from the present. If you anticipate the future, you are doing it now. The past is no more; the future is not yet. Only the now exists.

Science has embraced an orientation to process: the *how* of things taking place rather than the cause or the why of their taking place. Perls insisted that his clients concentrate on their awareness at each moment, of the details of what they were aware of, including feelings, posture, sensory data, and their actions. This is similar to mindfulness practice in Zen.

Perls believed that it is essential to draw patients' attention to their awareness of how they actually create the problem and how they prevent themselves from resolving it, rather than seeking useless answers to why they had the problem, which can waste years in therapy.

In Gestalt therapy, patients are guided to be more aware of their actual experience, including feelings, posture, expression, and actions. This inevitably leads patients into an impasse, the nothingness of the now, their center. Entering the void, they can be cured.

•

Morita Therapy

Morita therapy is a loose collection of approaches to psychological treatment used by students of Morita. Based on the work of Professor Shoma Morita, of Jikei University School of Medicine in Tokyo, Morita therapy utilizes psychiatric methods that fit the Japanese cultural character, and also draws from the resource of Zen for inspiration and direction. Similar to Zen, Morita therapy proposes that the self is an illusion; therefore, there is little concern for analysis of the problem. Instead, how to continue on with one's life and one's work is central. Morita therapy differs from most contemporary

Western therapies in which emotional release is emphasized. Emotion is background and inconsequential to Morita therapy. Returning to work and getting on with life is the main thing.

Similar to the practice of Zen, disciplined action is the Path. The patient's action is the focus. The Morita therapist does not inquire deeply into what is behind the troubling action, nor does he or she try to change it (this is an incorrect focus of effort and awareness). Instead, the Morita therapist draws the patient's attention to the actions themselves, not the effort, meaning intention or feelings, behind them. The therapist then asks the patient to simply continue working, to perform whatever is required, regardless of feelings or personal concerns. This situation calls upon patients to transcend their emotions.

Morita began his practice of therapy by helping patients in his own home, taking them in and giving them a calm, restful retreat or sanctuary in a warm family atmosphere.

Treatment was given in four stages. First, the patient remained in bed for absolute bed rest. No smoking, drinking, talking, reading, television viewing, etc., was allowed for a week. Forced to lie in bed, the patients sometimes found themselves obsessively ruminating over their problems and at other times obsessed with the wish to escape the situation. The burden of self-preoccupation might become unbearable. Morita would tell his patients that whatever they felt about the bed rest, they must do it anyway as their duty.

Light work was allowed in stage two. Patients kept a diary, did chores like sweeping, raking leaves, washing clothes. Little attention was given to the fleeting, ephemeral quality of feelings, coming and going like the seasons, considered to be unimportant. Instead, the tasks were the focus of attention.

Stage three involved heavier work like gardening, carpentry, cutting wood. Patients participated in group activities in which attitudes were addressed. For example, work is important to do not because people like it but rather because it is given. Patients were continually directed toward their work and not to their own feelings, motivations, or needs.

Re-entry into normal routines was the final stage, lasting for another week or so.

Morita therapy is an emotionally "cool" method of therapy, encouraging patients to lose themselves in work and in tasks instead of exploring their feelings. Like Zen, patients learn to let go of all the mental clutter to find a positive experience of mindfulness in work itself.

Morita therapists encourage patients to change their attitudes toward their circumstances and take constructive action in their lives, regardless of fears, worries, conflicts, or doubt. Difficulties disappear as action is taken, or at least, they cease to be the focus of the attention. Zen's simplicity and focus on action as a natural part of enlightenment is given form in Morita's approach. Morita therapy has something to teach us all about change.

•

Naikan Therapy

Another form of therapy that has emerged in Japan is known as Naikan therapy. Naikan therapy was created by Yoshimoto Ishin and his wife and co-therapist Yoshimoto Kinuko and amounts to a kind of study and confession of the ledger of the conscience, the daily social balance sheet of debits and credits, of what one has done right and what wrong. The word *Naikan* means inner (*nai*) observation (*kan*).

Naikan therapy lasts for a week, during which time patients partake of intensive study and self-reflection, from morning to night, recognizing what one has received from others, and what one has returned to others. The patients recognize with gratitude the love and support they have received and repent for their transgressions.

The *naikansha,* as a patient is called, sits behind a screen and meditates hour by hour, preparing for the *shidosha* (the guide or therapist) to come for *mensetsu* (the interview). Naikan may be performed with groups, but *mensetsu* is conducted individually. This form of therapy is applied to social deviants—prisoners, alcoholics, and juvenile delinquents—as well as for marriage and family counseling. The focus in proper Naikan is not just on the past but also on bringing about a change of heart, an enlightened Oneness with one's family, friends, and social group, and to sincerely express in everyday living these social virtues.

Naikan therapy insists on confession by the patient of wrongdoing with immersion in the personal feelings and moral self-judgments associated with transgression. In Western psychoanalysis, moral judgment is suspended during therapeutic exploration of feelings, thoughts, and actions. In Naikan therapy, moral judgment may be encouraged, even emphasized, along with self-disclosure. One Naikan therapist expressed this well: "It is quite proper that you should feel terrible in finding your faults." [3]

The intense scrutiny of actions with the *shidosha* in terms of guilt and social obligation can become almost unbearable at times. Zazen meditation can be used to help relieve excessive preoccupation with guilt by clearing the patient's mind between sessions with the *shidosha*.

Naikan assumes that we are all moral beings in our inner nature. Therapy aims to restore the balance.

> When we understand who we really are there is no need for external commands to do this or do that; rather, spontaneously, even joyfully we lose ourselves in the service of those around us. [4]

Some practitioners combine Zen practices with Naikan procedures. At Senkobo temple in Nara, Japan, the *shidosha* is also an ordained Zen Buddhist priest, Reverend Usami. His Naikan is practiced within the outer form of Zen Buddhism. Lectures on proper ways of behaving are given, including everything from daily politeness (such as opening and closing doors) to the moral obligations one has to others. There are also *dokusan* meetings (private Zen interviews) with the guide, Zen temple–style group chanting, meals in silence, with correct neatness, and even the Zen-like assistance from a slap with the *kyosaku* (flat stick) on the back to ensure correct meditation posture during *mensetsu*. The *naikansha* also engages in regularly spaced periods of meditative walking during the *mensetsu* in order to relieve the pain of sitting and to continue meditating.

Zen is also used in some Naikan establishments to relieve excessive obsessive guilt from overinvolvement in that facet of Naikan, to clear the mind. Thus, the focus can be returned to the important aspect of Naikan, a change of heart expressed in action, not just a depressing submergence in guilt, which would not be useful or therapeutic in itself.

Naikan encourages us all to live a life of balanced giving and receiving, to recognize the positive love and support that others have given in spite of our shortcomings, to respond with gratitude and even self-sacrificial action. In practical terms, do you open the door for others to pass, or shove through ahead of everyone? The self-centered ego submerges in Naikan reflection. As one patient said after Naikan therapy, "I believe that when I am discontented with daily life it shows I have neglected to reflect on myself." [5]

It is clear that Zen has found a home in psychotherapy, directly in philosophy and worldview—for example, in Gestalt therapy—and indirectly using Zen's customs, rituals, and procedures within the therapeutic regimes, as for example in Morita and Naikan therapy.

Zen's direct pointing to the inner nature dispels illusions and thus helps patients bypass conflicts and become one with their own inner nature, without a problem. Perceptions become clearer, the mind becomes more concentrated and focused, and the energy of life tends to become collected and gathered. Then, what needs to be done can be done. The mind, cleared by meditation, can recognize that anxiety, conflict, and struggle are part of life, not to be avoided but to be accepted and faced. When we realize this, we are in touch with our true nature.

Now Is *to* Be: Zen Exercises

Personality is seldom what it will become at first. So it can increase. . . . We tend to assume that this increase comes only from without, thus justifying the prejudice that one becomes a personality by stuffing into oneself as much as possible from outside. But the more assiduously we follow this recipe, the more stubbornly we believe that all increase has to come from without, the greater becomes our inner poverty. . . . Real increase of personality means consciousness of an enlargement that flows from inner sources.

—*Carl Gustav Jung*

Zen is based in a deep understanding of the wisdom of the inner mind, our Buddha-nature. When Zen masters take up a life of poverty, they disengage from all efforts to attain outer wealth and focus all their efforts on inner enrichment. The inner mind is where the true wealth resides. Over twenty-five hundred years, a long tradition of practice has evolved that is aimed solely at the inner mind. Always a personal experience, Zen begins and ends with you.

To Do
Is to Be:
Practicing Zen

ZEN HAS ALWAYS BEEN TAUGHT THROUGH ACTIVE
participation in one's own meditation. The exercises in this
section are drawn from Zen around the world; you will want
to experiment for yourself to determine which approach
works best for you. The exercises include traditional Zen
meditation rituals such as bowing, zazen, and koans. You will
find that you can make Zen links to your daily activity, bringing meditation into your everyday life.

Zen must always be experienced to be truly understood.
Theories and history are only shadows thrown by the light of
firsthand experiences bringing Zen to life. In the following
pages, you are invited to experiment with Zen and to make it
a part of your own life. Through Zen practice you can find a
wiser, more creative you: your own Buddha-nature that shines
brightly within.

Some of these exercises are drawn directly from the old
masters; others are modern adaptations. All allow you to try

Zen for yourself. If you like these exercises, you may decide to do more with Zen. You may wish to find a Zen center in your area. They will welcome you and offer you group support with many levels of involvement to fit your lifestyle and commitment. But Zen is also something you can practice individually; some of you may wish to develop on your own. Sincere practice, diligently pursued, is the surest path to enlightenment. There is a Path for everyone to follow.

•

Meditation

Meditation is the cornerstone of Zen. All practice aims at achieving a meditative state of mind that is aware and full of presence in the here and now.

The practice of Zen in the West has moved beyond the monastery to include laypeople who also wish to participate in the Zen experience. Meditation is a natural inroad for people from many faiths and varied backgrounds to practice Zen.

A meditation group

Today Zen includes several different types of meditation drawn from many of the ancient masters, originally taken from Buddha's enlightenment under the Bodhi tree, developed through the ages in the spirit of Zen, and brought to you today.

Each of these meditations has a different effect on the mind. Try them all to see which ones you find most helpful. Remember, ultimately the experience· is your own, rising up from within. Trust the process and enjoy!

Meditation on Breathing

Breathing has traditionally been a good place for the beginner to start with meditation. It can be very natural to focus your mind by following the breath.

• *Breathing Exercise 1*

Sit comfortably, cross-legged, on a small cushion. Keep your backbone straight yet not rigid. Place your hands across your lap, palms up, fingers open, with the back of the left hand resting on top of the right. Allow your thumbs to touch gently. The position should feel comfortable and open, allowing energy to flow freely around your body. Close your eyes and focus your attention on your breathing. Be aware as you breathe in and out. Allow the air to lift your rib cage slightly as you breathe in, then fall gently as you breathe out. Follow your breaths, in and out, in and out, for several minutes at first, until eventually you can remain quiet and focused for ten minutes.

• *Breathing Exercise 2*

Sit comfortably as in the previous exercise. Begin by focusing on your breathing. Now imagine that with each exhale, your mind empties of thoughts. Inhale then exhale air in regular breaths, not deep, and with each exhale let go of any distractions, tensions, or images. With each breath your mind can become clearer and calmer. Eventually you will find that what remains is a calm, clear, focused mental state.

Zazen

Zazen meditation, in the view of Dogen and the Soto School, is the single most important pathway to the Zen Way. Dogen told his students to devote themselves wholeheartedly to the endeavor—the rewards would be great:

> The mind, originally marvelous, clear, and bright suddenly emerges and the original light shines fully at last. [1]

Here are the instructions passed along from this great Soto master to you.

• *Zazen Exercise*

Find a place to practice zazen that is neither too hot nor too cold, neither too light nor too dark. You should not have eaten or drunk too much prior to a zazen session. Your clothing should be loose-fitting but neat. Spread a mat on the floor and then place a small pillow (usually rounded) on the mat to sit on.

Zazen uses a definite sitting position, dating back to the ancient Yogis. According to legend, this position was believed to be the sitting position that could conquer the devil. In postured sitting, your body finds a state of relaxed attention. Sit upright, cross-legged, as in the breathing exercises, with the left foot placed upon the right thigh and the right foot on the left thigh. If you find this uncomfortable, sit cross-legged with both feet resting on the floor. Place your hands palms up, with your right hand resting on the left foot and left hand resting on the right foot. If you are sitting in a modified cross-legged position, let the backs of your hands rest on your thighs. Your two thumbs should touch gently. Let your body be upright and straight but not rigid, with no leaning to left or right. Your head should be held straight, with your ears aligned over your shoulders. Let your tongue rest loosely against your palate and keep your lips and teeth closed. Eyes should be barely open.

Breathe calmly and regularly. As you begin to meditate, clear your mind of all thoughts. When a thought arises, notice it and then dismiss it, returning to your calm, clear mind. Continue to do this over time and you will eventually find that thoughts intrude less and less and that your concentration becomes natural and profound. Herein lies the Way to your Buddha-nature.

Koan

The Rinzai School approach to Zen meditation differs from the Soto School. Like Hui-neng, the Rinzai School believes that the Zen practitioner will suddenly have a profound enlightenment experience and be forever changed. Seekers must try fiercely, day and night, to see into their own nature.

Hakuin used koans in combination with meditation to bring about this experience. He thought the koan practice was important because the struggle creates a great tension within, leading to intense doubt of everything. Hakuin believed that at the bottom of great doubt lies great awakening. If you doubt fully, you will awaken fully.

Here is a typical koan that has been presented to students for centuries. Traditionally, this meditation did not require a quiet place. Whether you are in a quiet setting or a busy one should not matter. What is important is that you keep absolute focus on this koan.

Thinking About Not-Thinking

A monk asked Chao-chou (Joshū), "Does a dog have Buddha-nature? Chao-chou answered, "Mu." Now concentrate all your attention on Chao-chou's *Mu*. Ask what principle this *Mu* contains, but discard all emotions, concepts, and thoughts as you investigate it single-mindedly.

Chinese Soto Zen and some modern Soto schools have also incorporated koans, but always as a means to facilitate zazen. As Chinese monk named Yueh-shan Hung-tao sat quietly, a young disciple questioned him, "What do you think while sitting?"

The master answered, "Think of not-thinking."

Baffled, the student asked further, "How do you think of not thinking?"

The master's reply was simple, "Without thinking." With this in mind, try a modern koan.

• *Think of Nothing Exercise*

Sit comfortably and close your eyes. Now ask yourself this question: How can I think of nothing without thinking anything about it? If you think anything about it, you are not thinking of nothing. If you don't think anything about it, you are not thinking of nothing. How can you think of nothing? Can you? Let yourself become intrigued with the possibilities. Stay with it.

Meditative Walking

For centuries, monks have found that "just sitting" leads to sore legs, tired backs, and sleepy minds. They have instituted breaks in the staid, meditative posture without losing the focus of mind: by walking. Traditionally, meditative walking was done with the same precision as zazen, to guide Zen practitioners in continued clear mind. Once you are able to sustain your seated meditation for thirty minutes at a time, you should add breaks of meditative walking.

• *Traditional Meditative Walking Exercise*

Stand up with your hands folded together in front of your waist. Step out slowly with one foot, heel first, then roll forward to your toe. Next bring your other foot forward and carefully step, heel down, rolling forward to your toe. Walk slowly but smoothly, heel to toe. Keep your mind as clear as possible. Continue to do zazen as you walk. If you are with others, pick one person to lead. All others follow at the same pace. The leader should vary the pace, moving quicker and at other times moving slower again. Traditionally, meditators circle the outskirts of the meditation room. After a period of around fifteen minutes, sit down again and return to seated meditation.

• *Modern Meditative Walking Exercise*

For a modern variation, here is another form of walking meditation. Stand straight but relaxed, with your hands comfortably hanging at your sides. Close your eyes and allow your breathing to become relaxed. Walk as you would normally walk, but step much slower. Let yourself be relaxed as you walk. Keep your mind focused only on the walking. Notice how the floor feels on your feet, the air on your skin as you move. If you can do this out in nature, all the better. Notice all that you experience, but keep your mind only on walking. After approximately fifteen minutes of walking, return to your seated meditation.

Bowing

Bowing is another traditional way that is used to engage the mind and body in a meditative state. It is practiced in Korean and Japanese Zen centers today and was done by the ancient Chinese as well. Bowing, when done as a full prostration, can be very physical, so ease into it gradually. At the Kwan An School in Providence, Rhode Island, monks work up from 108 to as many as 1,080 bows a day, spread out over an entire day. (The number 108 is widely used as a significant number. The Shaolin monks had a hall of 108 wooden dummies as an ordeal for all to pass. Dogen had 108 ways of attaining enlightenment. The number 108 can be traced back to the Hindu 108 defilements of the mind.) For home practice, begin with as few as one or two and work your way up to 108. While you perform the movements, pay close attention to your physical experience and let no other thoughts carry you away.

• *Bowing Exercise*

Begin by standing with your feet together and hands pressed together, palms and fingers touching and pointing upward. There should be no gap between your hands. Hold your hands close to your body at mid-chest level. Next, drop gently to your knees, keeping your upper body as straight as possible, and sit on your heels. Keep your hands in the same position, palms and fingers touching. Rock back and then down to the floor, so that your forehead lightly touches the floor, your hands lying palms up on the floor next to your ears. Remain in this position for a few moments. Then rock forward to all fours, sit back on your heels, and straighten your back. Your hands move back together, palms and fingers touching, fingers up, close to your chest (as in the first hand position). Finally, stand straight up by pushing up with your leg muscles. Repeat.

•

Meditation in Daily Life: To Be All the Time

A day of no work is a day of no eating.

—Pai-chang

Zen practice has always included some type of daily labor. To truly practice Zen, you must bring it beyond the time spent in meditation and make it an integral part of daily life. If we are not able to apply it to daily life, then Zen has failed to be truly Zen. As D. T. Suzuki said:

As long as this meditation remains identified with abstractions, there will be no practical solution of the problem. . . . When this does not go beyond his hours of meditation, then it is not actually put to experiments in his daily life. The solution is merely ideational, it bears no fruits, and therefore it dies out before long. [2]

The main jobs required to keep a monastery running smoothly have usually been cleaning and farming. But Zen does not need to be restricted to any particular type of work.

In modern life, we are often called to do more abstract work in offices, stores, or services involving other people. We can approach any task with the mindful awareness achieved in meditation. Japanese Zen teaches us to make each activity an art. Our work refines itself and becomes the best it can be. The following exercises will help you apply your Zen skills to everyday life. You may find it helpful to work mindfully.

• *Meditation on a Task*

Pick something that you routinely do as part of your job. For your first time, choose a time-limited activity, such as typing, organizing, moving things, observing something, etc. Before you actually perform this meditation on the job, practice several times during meditation. Sit comfortably and close your eyes. Imagine yourself doing this task. Picture it vividly. Think through every detail, remembering what you experience when you work at it. Notice your usual mind-set and the physical aspects, what it feels like to perform this task.

Next time you are performing this task at your job, notice all the details as you do it. Can you put your full attention into this task without distraction? Let yourself perform it as well as you can, taking the extra moment to make it right. With time, you can broaden to many areas of your work, putting your attention on your work more fully. Do what you do well and fully attentive. With mindful work comes better quality work and often greater satisfaction for you!

• *Naikan Therapy Exercise*

Sit in a meditative posture, in quiet stillness. Examine your life for what you have received from others, and what you have given in return—the balance sheet of emotional obligations. How have you indebted yourself to others without realizing it? Can you acknowledge their love and support? Gratitude?

Now consider how you may not have met your obligations, how you may not be coming through for others in your life. How could you restore the balance? What actions could you do to help others? Can you plan how you could behave better in the future?

• *Awareness of Temperature Exercise*

Deepening your awareness can be done on a very concrete level with body temperature. This exercise can help you to stay more centered in the here and now. Raise your hand, holding your fingers together, and place your fingers in contact with your face at the top of your forehead. Feel the temperature. Now place your fingers in contact with your ear. Feel the temperature. How does it compare with the temperature of your forehead? Compare it with other areas of your face. Now roll up your sleeve. Place your fingers in contact with your other inner arm, down low near your wrist. Next, go to the elbow. Compare the temperature of your hand with that of your arm at the elbow. Now return to your ear and compare again, back and forth. Take the time to experience this. Your skin temperature actually varies over your body, and you probably have not noticed. In winter, the skin temperature may be lower at the ears, even indoors. In summertime there is less variation.

• *Be Fully Present in the Moment Exercise*

To be fully present, fully mindful in the moment, is true Zen. This exercise will help you enjoy and deepen your Oneness within and without.

Sit quietly in a natural setting where you will not be disturbed. Close your eyes and clear your mind. Give yourself the time it takes to stop all mind chatter and calm your mind. When you are ready, allow yourself to notice everything you experience in that moment. Are your muscles relaxed? Notice your sitting. How does your body meet the ground? Place your hands palms down on the earth. Can you feel how massive it is beneath you? Do you notice a breeze as it moves over your skin? Can you feel the air as it enters your nose and becomes part of your body? Is there sunshine warming you? How deeply does it penetrate? Do you hear birds singing? Allow yourself to experience all these things and more, mindful in this moment and at one with your environment. Enjoy!

EPILOGUE

A man grows with the greatness of his tasks.

—Carl Gustav Jung

ZEN CONTINUES ON ITS JOURNEY AROUND THE world, carrying a positive spirit that inspires us today. It is a phenomenon that not only has survived for twenty-five hundred years but continues to flourish anew. Why does Zen still speak to us today?

Zen has found a comfortable home through the ages in many countries. From the very first, Zen has attempted to step outside time and place, to communicate on a more fundamental level. Culture, language, customs, conventional reality are all viewed from a different perspective. It is true that Zen has inevitably taken on rituals of its own, often as outgrowths of the setting, like Pai-chang's monastic traditions, but ultimately these things can be set aside without compromising the true spirit of Zen.

Zen always reaches beyond the relative, into the regions of consciousness that touch human potential. How much can we know about the true nature of ourselves and reality? As Zen asks these questions here in the West, inevitably there will be interactions with the disciplines that ponder these issues, such as philosophy, psychology, and physics. Can we find answers to questions that our logic cannot answer? Zen points the way.

Zen seeks answers to life's questions deep within the individual. Zen practice discourages useless striving and turns you back to the wellsprings within your mind. True happiness and wealth can never come only from things outside yourself. Zen offers a corrective for the excesses of contemporary life.

Zen challenges you to discover your best innermost being. What you do with this discovery is up to you. Bodhidharma sat staring at a wall for nine years. Dogen was willing to give up every worldly possession down to the shirt on his back. We wonder what we personally do for the tasks our lives have presented us. Search deeply within your own being to find your life's higher task. The Zen Way points to deeper values that can help you realize your potential, unfolding in creative ways!

NOTES

CHAPTER 1 Awakening to Oneness: Zen Origins

1. Nirvana is freedom from suffering; samsara is the cycle of birth and death.
2. A koan is a question or puzzle presented to the student that requires a shift in consciousness to solve it. See pages 74–77 for further explanation.
3. Jacques Gernet, *A History of Chinese Civilization*, p. 295.
4. Wing-Tsit Chan, *Source Book in Chinese Philosophy*, p. 406.
5. Lankavatara Sutra, in D. T. Suzuki, *Manual of Zen Buddhism*, p. 53.
6. Edward Conze, *Buddhist Texts through the Ages*, p. 150.
7. Ibid., p. 151.
8. A. F. Price and Wong Mou-Lam, *The Diamond Sutra and The Sutra of Hui-Neng*, p. 24.
9. Ibid., p. 53.

CHAPTER 2 To Be Enlightened: Chinese Ch'an

1. Verse of the First Patriarch, in Philip Yampolsky, *The Platform Sutra of the Sixth Patriarch*, p. 62.
2. R. H. Blyth, *Zen and Zen Classics* (vol. I), pp. 100, 102.
3. Price & Mou-Lam, *The Diamond Sutra and The Sutra of Hui-Neng*, p. 70.
4. Ibid., p. 72.
5. Heinrich Dumoulin, *Zen Buddhism: A History*, p. 164.
6. Ibid., p. 165.
7. Ibid., p. 170.
8. John Blofeld, trans., *Zen Teachings of Huang Po*, p. 95.
9. Ibid., p. 108.
10. Ibid., p. 109.
11. Burton Watson, *The Zen Teachings of Master Lin-Chi*, p. 23.
12. Ibid., p. 15.
13. Ibid., p. 55.
14. Dumoulin, *Zen Buddhism: A History*, p. 234.
15. D. T. Suzuki, *The Zen Koan as a Means of Attaining Enlightenment*, p. 29.
16. Sekida Katsuki, *Two Zen Classics: Mumonkan and Hekiganroku*, and Paul Reps, *Zen Flesh, Zen Bones*.

CHAPTER 3 To Do and to Be Enlightened Are One: Japanese Zen

1. Lafcadio Hearn, *Japan, An Attempt at Interpretation,* p. 89.

2. Dumoulin, *Zen Buddhism: A History,* p. 27.

3. Yuho Yokoi, *Zen Master Dogen: An Introduction with Selected Writings,* p. 30.

4. See Chapter 10 for Dogen's explicit instructions on how to perform zazen.

5. Reiho Masunaga, *A Primer of Soto Zen,* p. 44.

6. Ibid., p. 62.

7. *Shobogenzo,* "Treasure Chamber of the Eye of True Dharma," the principal work of Master Dogen.

8. Yokoi, *Zen Master Dogen,* p. 163.

9. Dogen, in Yokoi, *Zen Master Dogen,* p. 84.

10. Dumoulin, *Zen Buddhism: A History,* p. 157.

11. Ibid., p. 163.

12. The Tokugawa era is also known as the feudal period in Japan.

13. Yamamoto Tsunetomo, *The Book of the Samurai: Hagakure,* p. 45.

14. Norman Waddell, *The Unborn: The Life and Teaching of Zen Master Bankei,* p. 79.

15. Ibid., p. 70.

16. Trevor Leggett, *A Second Zen Reader,* pp. 151–52.

17. Norman Waddell, *The Essential Teachings of Zen Master Hakuin,* p. xviii.

18. Leggett, *A Second Zen Reader,* p. 156.

19. Ruth Fuller Sasaki and Miura Isshu, *The Zen Koan: Its History and Use in Rinzai Zen,* p. 48.

20. Ibid., p. 50.

21. Sekida Katsuki, *Two Zen Classics: Mumonkan and Hekiganroku,* p. 171.

22. John Daido Loori, *Two Arrows Meeting in Mid-Air: The Zen Koan,* p. xxxix.

23. Ibid., p. . See the exercises in Chapter Ten for a description of Mu and an explanation of how to use it.

24. Hakuin, in Waddell, *The Essential Teachings of Zen Master Hakuin,* p. 103.

CHAPTER 4 To Be And To Do Are Not Two: Korean Son

1. Mu Soeng, *Thousand Peaks,* p. 37.

2. See Taesung Kishmon So, "Approaches to the Reconciliation of Doctrinal Controversy," *Treatise on Awakening of Faith* Taesung Kishinon Pyolki, (Special Commentary on the Awakening of Faith) and commentaries on many sutras such as the Wisdom Sutra, the Lotus Sutra, the Nirvana Sutra, Amitabha Sutra, and the Diamond Sutra.

3. Robert E. Buswell, *Tracing Back the Radiance,* p. 107.

4. J. C. Cleary, *A Buddha from Korea,* p. 77.

5. Mu Soeng, *Thousand Peaks,* p. 133.

6. Ibid., p. 128.

7. Robert E. Buswell, *The Zen Monastic Experience: Buddhist Practice in Contemporary Korea,* p. 30.

8. Mu Soeng, *Thousand Peaks,* p. 163.

CHAPTER 5 Transitions

1. D. T. Suzuki, *The Zen Doctrine of No-Mind*, p. 22.
2. Heinrich Dumoulin, *Zen Buddhism in the Twentieth Century*, p. 4.
3. D. T. Suzuki, *The Zen Koan as a Means of Attaining Enlightenment*, p. 30.
4. Helen Tworkov, *Zen in America: Five Teachers and the Search for an American Zen Buddhism*, p. 9.
5. Shunryu Suzuki, *Zen Mind, Beginner's Mind*, p. 58.
6. Ibid., p. 79.
7. "Shamon Dogen," in *Watsuji Tetsuro Zenshu*. (Collected Works of Watsuji Tetsuro).
8. Heinrich Dumoulin, *Zen Buddhism in the Twentieth Century*, p. 23.
9. Ibid., p. 25.
10. Descartes, *Discourse on Method and other Writings*, p. 53.
11. Christmas Humphreys, *A Western Approach to Zen*, p. 137.
12. R. H. Blyth, *Zen and Zen Classics*, p. 122.
13. Ibid., p. 123.
14. Eugene Herrigel, *Zen in the Art of Archery*, p. 85.
15. Gustie Herrigel, *Zen in the Art of Flower Arrangement*, p. 92.
16. Alan Watts, *The Way of Zen*, p. x.
17. Rudolf Otto in Dumoulin, *Zen Buddhism in the Twentieth Century*, p. 7.
18. Aelred Graham, *The End of Religion*, p. 264.
19. Paul Reps, *Zen Flesh, Zen Bones*, p. 114.
20. Maura O'Halloran, *Pure Heart, Enlightened Mind*, pp. 24–5.

CHAPTER 6 The Beats: On the Road to Enlightenment

1. Jack Kerouac, *The Dharma Bums*, p. 99.
2. John Clellon Holmes, "The Philosophy of the Beat Generation," in Seymour Krim, *The Beats*, p. 22.
3. Allen Ginsberg interview: "The Art of Poetry," *Paris Review* 10, no. 37, (spring, 1966), p. 47.
4. William Burroughs, "The Art of Fiction XXXVI," *Paris Review* 9, no. 35, (fall, 1965), p. 18.
5. Ginsberg, interview in Paul Portuges, *The Visionary Poetics of Allen Ginsberg*, p. 139.
6. Ibid.

CHAPTER 7 Mind Over Matter: Zen Arts

1. Herrigel, *Zen in the Art of Flower Arrangement*, p. 36.
2. A. L. Sadler, *Cha-no-yu: The Japanese Tea Ceremony*, p. 102.
3. D. T. Suzuki, *Zen and Japanese Culture*, p. 298.
4. Sadler, *Cha-no-yu*, p. 103.
5. Rikyu in Sadler, *Cha-no-yu*, p. 107.
6. Kakuzo Okakura, *The Book of Tea*, p. 109.
7. Herrigel, *Zen in the Art of Flower Arrangement*, p. 79.
8. Ibid., p. 16.
9. R. H. Blyth, *Haiku*, p. 270.
10. Bashō in Harold G. Henderson, *Haiku in English*, p. 24.

11. Bashō in Nancy Ross, *The World of Zen*, p. 125.

12. Bashō in Henderson, *Haiku in English*, p. 18.

13. Suzuki, *Zen and Japanese Culture*, p. 254.

14. Ross, *The World of Zen*, p. 112.

15. Ibid., p. 112.

16. Henderson, *Haiku in English*, p. 14.

17. Hackett in Henderson, *Haiku in English*, p. 30.

18. Ibid.

19. Ross, *The World of Zen*, p. 120.

20. Seami Motokiyo in Arthur Waley, *The Nō Plays of Japan*, p. 44.

21. Ibid., pp. 15–59.

22. Ross, *The World of Zen*, p. 180.

23. Seami Motokiyo in Waley, *The Nō Plays of Japan*, p. 44.

24. Mas Oyama, *The Kyokushin Way.*

25. Ibid., p. 68.

26. Timothy W. Gallway, *The Inner Game of Tennis*, p. 108.

27. Herrigel, *Zen in the Art of Archery*, p. 35.

CHAPTER 8 To Be Is to Act: Zen Activism

1. Dumoulin, *Zen Buddhism: A History, India and China*, p. 32.

2. Su Bong, *Primary Point*, vol. 11, no. 1, p. 12.

3. Bob Maat and Liz Bernstein, *Primary Point*, vol. 10, no. 2, p. 7.

4. Thich Nhat Hanh, *Love in Action*, p. 47.

5. Ibid., p. 81.

6. Ibid., p. 101.

7. Ibid., p. 129.

8. Joanna Macy, "Technology & Mindfulness" *Mountain Record.* XII, no. 3 (spring 1994), p. 44.

CHAPTER 9 Being Whole: Zen and Psychotherapy

1. Frederick S. Perls, *Gestalt Therapy Verbatim*, p. 57.

2. Ibid., p. 40.

3. Yoshimoto Ishin, in David Reynolds, *Naikan Psychotherapy*, p. 105

4. Yamamoto in Reynolds, *Naikan Psychotherapy:*, p. 90.

5. Ibid., p. 5.

CHAPTER 10 To Do Is to Be: Practicing Zen

1. Dumoulin, *Zen Buddhism: A History of Japan*, p. 77.

2. D. T. Suzuki, *Training of the Zen Buddhist Monk*, pp. 33–34.

BIBLIOGRAPHY

Abe, Masao. *Buddhism and Interfaith Dialogue.* Honolulu: University of Hawaii Press, 1995.

———. *Zen and Western Thought.* Honolulu: University of Hawaii Press, 1985.

Beck, L. A. *The Story of Oriental Philosophy.* New York: New Home Library, 1928.

Blyth, R. H. *Zen and Zen Classics* (2 vols.). San Francisco: Hokuseido Press, 1960, 1964.

———. *Haiku* (4 vols.) Tokyo: The Hokuseido Press, 1947.

Burroughs, William. "The Art of Fiction XXXCI." *Paris Review* 9, no. 35, (1965).

Buswell, Robert E. *Tracing Back the Radiance.* Honolulu: University of Hawaii Press, 1983.

———. *The Zen Monastic Experience: Buddhist Practice in Contemporary Korea.* Princeton, N. J.: Princeton University Press, 1992.

Chan, Wing-Tsit. *A Source Book in Chinese Philosophy.* Princeton, N. J.: Princeton University Press, 1963.

Cleary, J. C. *A Buddha From Korea.* Boston: Shambhala, 1988.

Conze, Edward. *Buddhism.* New York: Philosophical Library, 1951.

———. *Buddhist Texts through the Ages.* New York: Philosophical Library, 1954.

———. *Buddhist Wisdom Books.* London: George Allen and Unwin Ltd., 1958.

Creel, Herlee G. *Chinese Thought from Confucius to Mao Tse-Tung.* Chicago: University of Chicago Press, 1953.

Dumoulin, Heinrich. *Zen Buddhism: A History* (2 vols.). New York: Macmillan, 1988, 1990.

———. *Zen Buddhism in the Twentieth Century.* New York: Weatherhill, 1992.

———. *Zen Enlightenment: Origins and Meaning.* New York: Weatherhill, 1979.

Eliot, Sir Charles. *Hinduism and Buddhism* (3 vols.). New Delhi: Mehra Offset Press, 1988.

Fitzgerald, C. P. *China, A Short Cultural History.* New York: Frederick A. Praeger, 1954.

———. *A Concise History of East Asia.* New York: Frederick A. Praeger, 1967.

Furlong, Monica. *Merton, A Biography.* San Francisco: Harper and Row, 1948.

Gallway, Timothy W. *The Inner Game of Tennis.* New York: Bantam, 1979.

———. *Inner Tennis: Playing the Game.* New York: Random House, 1976.

Gernet, Jacques. *A History of Chinese Civilization.* Cambridge, England: Cambridge University Press, 1996.

Ginsberg, Allen and Andrei Voznesernsky. "A Conversation." *Paris Review* 22, no. 78 (1980).

———. "The Art of Poetry VIII." *Paris Review* 10, no. 37 (1966).

Goodman, Paul. *Growing Up Absurd.* New York: Vintage, 1960.

Graham, Dom Aelred. *Zen Catholicism.* New York: Harcourt, Brace Jovanovich, Inc., 1963.

———. *The End of Religion.* New York: Harcourt Brace Jovanovich, Inc., 1971.

Hanh, Thich Nhat. *Love in Action.* Berkeley, Calif.: Parallax Press, 1993.

Hearn, Lafcadio. *Glimpses of Unfamiliar Japan.* Rutland, Vt.: Charles E. Tuttle Co., Inc., 1967.

———. *Japan, An Attempt at Interpretation.* New York: Grosset & Dunlap, 1904.

Henderson, Harold G. *Haiku in English.* Rutland, Vt.: Charles E. Tuttle Co., Inc., 1967.

Herrigel, Eugene. *The Method of Zen.* New York: Vintage, 1960.

———. *Zen in the Art of Archery.* New York: Vintage, 1971.

Herrigel, Gustie. *Zen in the Art of Flower Arrangement.* London: Penguin, 1958.

Hucker, Charles O. *China's Imperial Past.* Stanford, Calif.: Stanford University Press, 1975.

Humphreys, Christmas. *A Western Approach to Zen.* Wheaton, Ill.: Theosophical Publishing House, 1971.

Hyams, Joe. *Zen in the Martial Arts.* Los Angeles: J. P. Tarcher, 1979.

Jung, Carl. *Archetypes and the Collective Unconscious.* Princeton, N. J.: Princeton University Press, 1969.

———. *Psychology and the East.* Princeton, N. J.: Princeton University Press, 1978.

Kapleau, Philip. *Zen Dawn in the West.* Garden City, N.Y.: Anchor Books, 1980.

Kerouac, Jack. *The Dharma Bums.* New York: Penguin, 1972.

———. *On the Road.* New York: Penguin, 1976.

Krim, Seymour. *The Beats.* Greenwich, Conn.: Fawcett, 1960.

LaFleur, William R. *Dogen Studies.* Honolulu: University of Hawaii Press, 1985.

Lee, Bruce. *The Tao of Jeet Kune Do.* Burbank, Calif.: Ohara, 1975.

Leggett, Trevor. *A Second Zen Reader.* Rutland, Vt.: Charles E. Tuttle Co., Inc., 1988.

Loori, John Daido. *Two Arrows Meeting in Mid-Air: The Zen Koan.* Boston: Charles E. Tuttle Co., Inc., 1994.

Luk, Charles. *The Secrets of Chinese Meditation.* York Beach, Maine: Samuel Weiser, 1969.

Masunaga, Reiho. *A Primer of Soto Zen.* Honolulu: University of Hawaii Press, 1971.

Merton, Thomas. *Mystics and Zen Masters.* New York: Noonday Press, 1967.

———. *The Seven Storey Mountain.* New York: Harcourt Brace Javanovich, 1948.

———. *Zen and the Birds of Appetite.* New York: New Directions, 1968.

Merzel, Dennis. *Beyond Sanity and Madness: The Way of Zen Master Dogen*. Boston: Charles E. Tuttle Co., Inc., 1994.

Nitobe, Inazo. *Bushido: The Soul of Japan*. Rutland, Vt.: Charles E. Tuttle Co., Inc., 1969.

O'Halloran, Maura. *Pure Heart, Enlightened Mind*. Boston: Charles E. Tuttle Co., Inc., 1994.

Oyama, Mas. *The Kyokushin Way*. Tokyo: Japan Publications, 1979.

Okakura, Kakuzo. *The Book of Tea*. Tokyo: Kodansha, 1989.

Perls, Frederick S. *Gestalt Therapy Verbatim*. Lafayette, Calif.: Real People Press, 1969.

Pine, Red. *The Zen Teachings of Bodhidharma*. San Francisco: North Point Press, 1989.

Portuges, Paul. *The Visionary Poetics of Allen Ginsberg*. Santa Barbara, Calif.: Ross-Erikson Publishers, 1978.

Price, A. F. and Wong Mou-Lam. *The Diamond Sutra and The Sutra of Hui-Neng*. Boston: Shambhala, 1990.

Reps, Paul. *Morita Psychotherapy*. Berkeley, Calif.: University of California Press, 1976.

———. *Zen Flesh, Zen Bones*. Boston: Charles E. Tuttle Co., Inc., 1994.

Reynolds, David. *Naikan Psychotherapy: Meditation for Self-Development*. Chicago: University of Chicago Press, 1983.

———. *Playing Ball on Running Water: Living Morita Psychotherapy: The Japanese Way to Building a Better Life*. New York: Quill, 1984.

Ross, Nancy. *The World of Zen*. New York: Vintage Books, 1960.

Sadler, A. L. *Cha-no-yu: The Japanese Tea Ceremony*. Rutland, Vt.: Charles E. Tuttle Co., Inc., 1967.

Sansom, G. B. *Japan, A Short Cultural History*. New York: Appleton-Century-Crofts, 1962.

Sasaki, Ruth Fuller and Miura Isshu. *The Zen Koan: Its History and Use in Rinzai Zen*. San Diego: Harcourt, Brace, Jovanovich, 1965.

Sekida, Katsuki. *Two Zen Classics: Mumonkan and Hekiganroku*. New York: Weatherhill, 1977.

Shibayama, Abbot Zenkei. *A Flower Does Not Talk: Zen Essays*. Rutland, Vt.: Charles E. Tuttle Co., Inc., 1970.

Shimano, Edo T. *Points of Departure: Zen Buddhism with a Rinzai View*. Livingston Manor, N.Y.: Zen Studies Society Press, 1991.

Soeng, Mu. *Thousand Peaks*. Berkeley, Calif.: Parallax Press, 1987.

Suzuki, D. T. *Essays in Zen Buddhism* (first series). New York: Grove Press, 1978.

———. *Essays in Zen Buddhism* (third series). London: Rider & Co., 1953.

———. *Manual of Zen Buddhism*. New York: Grove Weidenfeld, 1960.

———. *Training of the Zen Buddhist Monk*. Boston: Charles E. Tuttle Co., Inc., 1994.

———. *The Zen Doctrine of No-Mind*. York Beach, Maine: Samuel Weiser, Inc. , 1972.

———. *Zen and Japanese Culture*. Princeton, N. J.: Princeton University Press, 1973.

————. *The Zen Koan as a Means of Attaining Enlightenment.* Boston: Charles E. Tuttle Co., Inc., 1994.

Suzuki, Shunryu. *Zen Mind, Beginner's Mind.* New York: Weatherhill, 1979.

Taylor, Eugene. *William James on Exceptional Mental States.* New York: Charles Scribner's Sons, 1982.

Tworkov, Helen. *Zen in America: Five Teachers and the Search for an American Zen Buddhism.* New York: Kodansha International Press, 1994.

Waddell, Norman, trans. *The Essential Teachings of Zen Master Hakuin.* Boston: Shambhala, 1994.

————. *The Unborn: The Life and Teachings of Zen Master Bankei.* San Francisco: North Point Press, 1984.

Waley, Arthur. *The Nō Plays of Japan.* New York: Grove Press, Inc., date unknown.

Watson, Burton. *The Zen Teachings of Master Lin-Chi.* Boston: Shambhala, 1993.

Watts, Alan. *Psychotherapy East and West.* New York: Vintage, 1975.

————. *This Is It.* New York: Vintage, 1973.

————. *The Way of Zen.* New York: Vintage, 1957.

Whitmyer, Claude, ed. *Mindfulness and Meaningful Work: Explorations of Right Livelihood.* Berkeley, Calif.: Parallax Press, 1994.

Yokoi, Yuho. *Zen Master Dogen: An Introduction with Selected Writings.* New York: Weatherhill, 1990.

Yampolsky, Philip B. *The Platform Sutra of the Sixth Patriarch.* New York: Columbia University Press, 1967.

GLOSSARY

NOTE: The number following each entry indicates the page number(s) where the term is first discussed in the text.

Amida Buddhism follows the school of Chinese Buddhism whose goal is to be reborn in the pure land of Amitabha by way of the recitation of his name. 32–33

Ananda was Buddha's disciple and personal attendant, known for having repeated all of the Buddha's discourses from memory at the First Council, where they were recorded. 11

Arhat is a perfected saint, one who has reached nirvana in Hinayana Buddhism through ascetic denial of worldly life. 12

Asanga developed the Yogacara School in the fourth century A.D. with his brother Vasubandu. 20

Asoka was a legendary king of India in the second century B.C who became a strong advocate of Buddhism following his conversion. 14

Avatamsaka Sutra is a large collection of Mahayana sutras that is the basis of the Chinese Hua-yen (Kegon Jap.) School of Buddhism. 38–40

Bankei (1622–93) was a Rinzai monk whose straightforward talks appealed to large numbers of people. He encouraged people to stay in the Unborn Mind. 110–112

Bashō (1643–94), known as the First Pillar of Haiku, was one of the greatest Zen haiku poets. 180–181

Bodhi tree is the fig tree under which the historical Buddha, Siddhartha Gautama, attained complete enlightenment. 8

Bodhidharma (c. 470–543)was the twenty-eighth Dharma descendant of Shakyamuni Buddha. Bodhidharma was the Indian monk who brought Zen to China, where he became known as the First Patriarch of Zen. 42–48

Bodhisattva is the enlightened exemplar in Mahayana Buddhism, one who practices the Buddha Way and compassionately foregoes final enlightenment for the sake of helping others to become enlightened. 15

Buddha (Awakened One) is a term that variously indicates the historical Buddha, Siddhartha Gautama, and also refers to any enlightened persons who have attained Buddhahood. 7–11

Ch'an is the Chinese word for Zen. 42–77

Cha-no-yu is the tea ceremony practiced as a Zen art. 172–177

Chao-chou Ts'ung-shen (Jap. Joshu, 778–897) was one of the Zen masters of China during the T'ang dynasty. He is mentioned many times in the *Mumonkan* koan stories. 61

Chih-i (538–97) was the Fourth Patriarch of the T'ien-t'ai School of Chinese Buddhism, but is often considered the founder because of his many clearly written treatises on T'ien-t'ai. 29–30

Chinul (1158–1210) was an important Korean Zen monk who helped unify Zen schools with Doctrinal Buddhist schools. He combined sudden enlightenment with gradual cultivation in his theory. 128–131

Chogye Order was formed in 1356 when the Nine Mountain Zen Schools of Korea were organized by T'aego into one order. 133–134

Daitoku-ji (Great Virtue) was the line of Rinzai Zen, founded by Shuho and originating from the lineage of Nampo. It became one of the influential Rinzai lines in Japan. 88

Daruma is a Japanese word for Bodhidharma. It was also a small sect of Zen where Ejo, a disciple of Dogen, first studied Buddhism. 98

Dharma is the universal truth or law. It is a word broadly used to refer to Buddha's teachings. 10

Dharmakaya koans (hossin koans) are the first level of Hakuin's koan system, concerned with the realization of universal unity. 117

Dharmaraksha (A.D. 231–308) translated more than 175 Buddhist works to help introduce Indian Buddhism to the Chinese. 25

Diamond Sutra, written around A.D. 350, is a small book in the Prajnaparamita sutra collection that epitomizes Zen's message of wordless insight beyond thought and reason. 37–38

Dogen (1200–53), founder of the Japanese Soto school of Zen, has had a profound and lasting influence on Zen. 90–99

Dosho (629–700) learned Zen from Hui-man in China and opened the first meditation hall in Japan. 84

Duk Sung Son, one of the founding fathers of modern Tae Kwon Do, brought this Korean martial art to America in the 1960s. 189

Eicho (d. 1247) was one of Ei-sai's disciples who remained in Japan to carry on Eisai's teachings. Eicho was also a Tendai monk. 86

Eightfold Path the content of the Buddha's fourth noble truth; the way out of suffering is through right views, right determination, right speech, right action, right livelihood, right effort, right mindfulness, and right concentration. 10

Eisai (Myoan 1141–1215) is considered the first Japanese monk to transmit an enduring Zen tradition to Japan. He founded the first Rinzai monastery and was also one of Dogen's teachers. 85–86

Enlightenment in Zen is the direct experience of one's true nature.

Enni Ben'en (1201–80) was a pivotal monk of thirteenth-century Japan. He had one of the Five Mountain Temples built at Tofuku-ji where he served as abbot. 87–88

Fa-hsien (337–422) traveled to India to obtain Buddhist texts and wrote about his adventures in a book, *Fo-kuo chi,* or *The Travels of Fa-hsien.* 27

Fa-tsang (643–712) was the Third Patriarch of the Hua-yen School, and considered by many to be its most important

contributer, writing more than sixty works on the philosophy. 31

Fa-yen School (House of Hogen) was one of the Five Houses of Zen in China. Fa-yen Wen-i (Jap. Hogen Bun'eki, 885–958) founded the school, which offered a gentler approach than the other four houses. 72

Five Ranks is a complex formula that gives a step-by-step pathway to enlightenment. It is based on the belief that there is no fundamental difference between insights obtained in meditation and those gained through study. 69–70

Four Noble Truths are the first teachings of Buddha that address the nature of suffering and point the way to overcome suffering. 9–10

Fun'yoroku (Ch. Fan-yang-lu) was the earliest systematic koan collection. It consisted of three volumes and was written by Fen-yang (947–1024). 75

Gasan Jito (1727–97) played an important part in bringing Hakuin-Zen into the modern era. 119

Gasan Jōseki (1275–1365) brought Soto Zen to the rural population, introducing the idea of social conscience into the practice of Soto Zen. 106

Gestalt Therapy is a form of psychotherapy based on German Gestalt psychology that also utilizes Zen's idea of emptiness, 204–206

Goi is the fifth level koans of Hakuin that incorporates the Five Ranks of Tung-shan. See Five Ranks. 118

Gonsen is the third level in the classification of Rinzai koans created by Hakuin, requiring students to use words to free the mind. 118

Gozan were the Five Mountain Temples, part of institutionalized Zen in Japan (1200–1600). The three-tiered system also included Ten Temples (jissetsu) and many larger temples (shozan) headquartered in Kyoto and Kamakura. 99–100

Graham, Dom Aelred was one of the first Catholics of the twentieth century to write about the connection between Eastern and Western religions. 158–159

Gyoyu (1163–1241) was one of Eisai's two disciples who combined Zen with Buddhism in his teachings. He spent his later years as abbot of Eisai's temple, Jufuku-ji. 86

Hagakure is a collection of writings concerning the way of the samurai. The author, Yamamoto Tsunetomo, wrote it around 1716. 108

Hakuin Ekaku (1685–1768) was the Patriarch of Japanese Rinzai Zen, through whom all present-day Rinzai masters have their lineage. 112–120

Hakuin Yasutani (1885–1973) was brought to America to carry on the introduction of Zen in America. He blended Soto with Rinzai. 146

Hekiganroku (Blue Cliff Record) was composed about one hundred years earlier than the *Mumonkan.* This koan collection is based on one hundred koans compiled by the poet-monk Hsueh-tou Ch'ung-hsien (980–1052). 76–77

Herrigel, Eugen (d. 1955) and **Gustie** (1887–1974) went to Japan together and learned Zen arts. They then wrote commentaries on Zen, helping to clarify the Zen experience for Westerners. 155–156

Hinayana Buddhism derives from the original Old Wisdom

School of Buddhism. Practitioners strive for the pure, enlightened life of the arhat. It has remained popular in Southeast Asia and Sri Lanka. 12–14

Ho-tse Shen-hui (Jap. Kataku Jinni, 670–762) was the Seventh Patriarch of the Southern School. He probably did more than anyone else to launch the Southern School's dominance and derail the Northern School's popularity. 57

"Hsinhsinming" ("Inscribed on the Believing Mind") is considered the first Zen poem. It was written by the Third Partiarch, Seng-ts'an. 50

Hua-yen (Jap. Kegon School) was a syncretic school of Buddhism that became a large movement in China. 31–32

Huang-po (Jap. Obaku, d. 850) was the monk who taught Lin-chi (Rinzai) along with thousands of others. 62–63

Hui-k'o (Jap. Eka, 487–593) was the Second Zen Patriarch; in Zen lore, he cut off his arm and presented it to Bodhidharma to prove his earnestness as a student. 45–46

Hui-neng (Jap. Eno, 638–713) was the Sixth Patriarch and author of the Platform Sutra. He was the first to teach sudden enlightenment. 54–58

Hui-yuan (334–416) was the founder of the Pure Land (Amida) Sect in China. (see Amida) 32

Hung-chih Cheng-chueh (1091–1157) was the leader of the Soto line during the Sung Period in China when Zen consolidated into two major traditions: Soto and Rinzai. 74

Hung-jen (Jap. Gunin, 601–74) was the Fifth Chinese Patriarch of Zen and is best remembered for the many students he in-

spired, including Hui-neng. 51–52

Hwa Rang Do (the Flower of Youth) was an elite corps of Silla (now Korea) warrior knights who trained in martial arts, philosophy, and a strict code of chivalry. 125

Ikebana is the Japanese Zen art of flower arranging. 177–180

I-k'ung (Jap. Giku) was invited by the Empress Tachibana Kachiko (834–84) to teach Zen in a temple she built, but he gave up and left, leaving an inscription on the wall at Rashoman: Zen will never be propagated to the East. 84

Imakita Kosen (1816–92) was the teacher of Shaku Soen, the monk who opened Zen to the West. Kosen found unity between Confucianism, Buddhism, Taoism, and Shinto. 122

Indra's Net is a description of the universe presented in the Avatamsaka Sutra that clearly displays the interconnections and interdependence of all things. 39

Inzan Ien (1751–1814) was a disciple of Gasan (Hakuin's disciple) who began one of the two modern branches of Hakuin-Zen. He was confrontational in his methods. 121–122

Jimmutennu (660 B.C.) was the legendary emperor of Japan who was said to be descended from the sun goddess, justifying the tradition of worshiping the emperor. 79

Jissetsu were the Ten Temples in the Japanese Temple-Monastery system. 99

Ju-ching (Jap. Nyojo, 1163–1238) was one of Dogen's teachers. 91–92

Kakushin (1207–98) was one of Gyoyu's students who studied with Wu-men and brought his

Mumonkan back from China to Japan. 86–87

Kami refers to the Shinto spirits. 109

Kanzan Egen (1277–1360) was a student of Shujo who was given a temple by Emperor Hanazono. 105

Kegon School (see Hua-yen)

Kennin-ji Monastary, founded in 1202, was one of the two Zen monasteries in Japan where Eisai served as abbot. 85

Kikan is the second level of the Rinzai koans created by Hakuin related to unity and multiplicity. 117

Koan is an apparently paradoxical statement or question used in Zen training to induce in students an intense level of doubt. This helps them cut through conventional and conditioned descriptions of reality and see directly into their true nature. 74–77

Koun Ejo (1198–1280) was Dogen's successor who carried on his master's teachings. 97–98

Kuei-yang School (House of Igyo) was one of the Five Houses of Zen in China that taught through experience.

Kuei-shan Liang-yu (Jap. Isan Reiyu, 771–853) was the founder of this school and student of Pai-chang. 70–71

Kumarajiva (344–413) supervised hundreds of monks in translating ninety-four Buddhist works from Sanskrit to Chinese at his bureau of translation. 25–26

Kyo is the doctrinal school in Korea that believed in the importance of sutra studies and traditional Buddhist rituals. 128–131

Lankavatara Sutra emphasizes the psychological aspects of the process of enlightenment by describing the states of consciousness involved. 35–36

Lin-chi (Jap. Rinzai Gigen, d. 866) is considered the founding father of Rinzai Zen. 64–66

Madhyamika, the Middle Way, is the school of Buddhism originated by Nagarjuna in the second century. 17–19

Mahakasyapa (also Kasyapa) became the Dharma successor of Buddha. 10–11

Mahasanghika was an innovative dissenting Old Wisdom School of Buddhism, beginning around 250 B.C. This school was the forerunner of Mahayana Buddhism. 15

Mahayana Buddhism was the newer form of Buddhism that developed during the first century A.D. It expresses and aims at the intrinsic connection between an individual's realization and the simultaneous enlightenment of all beings. 14–19

Mang Gong (1872–1946) opened his monastery doors to everyone. He taught Seung Sahn, the Korean monk who brought Korean Zen to America. 137

Ma-tsu (Jap. Baso Doitsu 709–88) was the first Zen monk known to use shouting and shock to foster enlightenment. His great intensity and spontaneity helped set the tone for Zen's growth during the T'ang period. 59–60

Merton, Thomas (1915–68) was a Trappist monk whose books and lectures helped promote the interaction between Zen and Christianity. 159

Mokichi Shuko (1453–1502) was the first Zen monk to find enlightenment through tea and become recognized as a tea master. 174

Morita Therapy is a form of psychotherapy that integrates

psychiatric techniques with Zen Buddhism. 206–208

Mumonkan (Ch. *Wu-men Kuan, The Gateless Gate*) is a major collection of koans consisting of forty-eight cases and is considered a primary source of Zen koans. 76–77

Muso (1275–1351) was a National Teacher of Zen in Japan who oversaw the building of the temple-monastery system. 100–102

Myoshin-ji was the temple built by Emperor Hanazono on his estate for Shoho's student, Kanzan. Even though it was small and somewhat run-down, many prominent Zen masters studied there, including Hakuin. 105

Myozen was the student and dharma succesor of Eisai and one of Dogen's teachers. 86

Nagarjuna was an Indian monk philosopher and logician who detailed and elucidated a philosophy of emptiness and the middle way based on paradoxical logic. 17–19

Naikan Therapy is a method of therapy that guides people to search inward for deep self-reflection. 208–211

Nakagawa Soen (1907–84) was a Japanese Zen monk who helped Americans link Zen to Western culture. 145–146

Nampo Shōmyō (1235–1309) was an early Japanese Zen monk who influenced Japanese practitioners to make Zen "Japanese" instead of viewing it as a foreign "Chinese" philosophy. 88

Nanto is the fourth level of koans created by Hakuin referring to the use of mystery. 118

Nan-yuan Hui-yung (Jap. Nanin Egyo, d. 930) was the first Zen monk to use koans. 74–75

Nishida Kitaro (1870–1945)

founded the Kyoto School, devoted to the interaction between Eastern and Western philosophy, including Zen. 151–152

Nishitani Keiji (1900–1990) was a member of the Kyoto School, who dedicated his life to enhancing the dialogue between East and West in philosophy. 152–153

Northern School in China emphasized calm meditative practice without concern for sudden enlightenment. 52–54

Nyogen Senzaki (1876–1958) was one of the first Zen masters to settle in America and stay, teaching Zen to Americans. 145

Oda Nobunaga (1534–82) launched a comprehensive campaign to eradicate Buddhism from Japan. 107

Old Wisdom School, now known as Hinayana, was the first school of Buddhism. 12–14

Otto, Rudolf (1867–1930) was a German theologian specializing in comparative religions, East and West. 157–158

Pai-chang (Jap. Hyakujo Ekai, 720–824) established the rules of Zen monastic life that are followed today. 61–62

Platform Sutra contains the biography, discourses, and sayings of the Sixth Chinese Zen Patriarch Hui-neng. 54

Prajna is enlightened wisdom that transcends duality of subject and object. 143

Prajnaparamita (Perfect Wisdom) is a large body of Mahayana sutras with the underlying message that enlightenment leads to perfect wisdom. The Diamond Sutra and Heart Sutra are two of the best known. 36–38

Precepts (Skt. sila; Jap. kai) are